The
Mind
of
Thuse!!

Thriving Within Effortlessness

The
Mind
of
Thuse!!

Thriving Within Effortlessness

Linda S. Smarzik

A ONE BREATH VILLAGE PUBLICATION | PUBLISHED BY ONE BREATH VILLAGE, LLC
www.onebreathvillage.com

Printed in the United States of America
First published in 2013

ISBN - 978-0-9843674-4-3

COVER ILLUSTRATION BY JENNY HSIAO

EDITED BY ANYA GROSSMAN AND
MARLA QUICK

FINAL EDIT BY CAMILLE DeSALME

BOOK PRODUCTION BY
MARK GELOTTE

AUTHOR PHOTOGRAPH BY KOREY HOWELL

For my grandmother
Mary M. Miller

My modern day mystic, hero, and saint—all rolled into a rebellious little rascal

Contents

THANK YOU, THANK YOU, THANK YOU!

A whole lot of help, love, and support is what it took to publish
this work. First and foremost, thank you to my editors: *Anya Grossman*
and *Marla Quick*. We jokingly talked about how we became our
own Triangle of Thuse—each needing the other to complete the task
at hand! Anya was able to clearly see the trees in the forest and thus
helped to communicate the message—the how, what, and why. Her
work is flawless. Her attention to detail is outstanding. Her service is
unending. Anya's positive and realistic outlook carried the writing into a
professional and polished body of work. Thank you, Anya!

And then ... there is Marla. She could see the forest of this
work by understanding the concepts right side up and upside down. She
has practiced the precepts of the Triangle of Thuse for years. At times,
she's revealed aspects to me that I would have simply missed. Countless
hours of conversation and structural editing helped to construct the
very premise of this work. Marla, you know my gratitude is unending.

Of course, any written work needs that final, final, final edit.
That is when Camille DeSalme came into the picture. Her eye for
catching those tiny mistakes just blew us all away. Thank you Camille.

Thank you to *Chris Burns* who said yes to anything I put on
her desk. If she did not know how to do the task, she fearlessly figured
it out—countless times. Thank you *Ann Kennedy* for the three (maybe
four) semesters of putting together the student pilot versions of hand-
bound, laminated, hole-punched, previous editions of this work. Your
support and prodding helped to publish the work "for real." *Jenny,
Jenny, Jenny Hsiao*, thank for your brilliance with the illustration for
the front cover. That illustration is a beautiful concept and rendition and
... I am forever grateful for our friendship. *Ernest Gregg*, thank you for
your coding brilliance. How many times did I get stuck on that website
and you came in to rescue? Who could be without *Mark Gelotte*, who
patiently walked me through "getting the files ready" and then double
and triple checking them before going to the printer.

And then there is *Stephanie Barko*—an amazing literary publicist who has revealed many of the mysterious aspects of this publishing world. Don't try to publish without a Stephanie Barko.

Mary Jane Holland. I am forever grateful for our many hours of talking, healing, crying, support, and laughter. You believed in this work before I did. Your gifts and talent still amaze me.

And thank you to my siblings with their ongoing, nonstop support: my sisters, *Beth Smarzik* and Nancy *Strowd*, and brother, *Richard Smarzik*. Lots of conversations with them were punctuated by "you can do it!" "go, Linda, go!" I have the best siblings in the universe.

Thank you to my *mom, Kathleen Smarzik,* for never giving up on us kids. We wish you were here to see how lovely your kids and grandkids turned out. You would like that.

And to my grandmother, *Mary M. Miller,* you were my modern day mystic, hero, and saint rolled into unconventional rebelliousness. I'll never forget the day when you tried to race us in your red Malibu. I knew I would forever love the rebel in you.

Thank you to the Barker family: *Rita* and *Keith Barker*, *Sabrina* and *Tristan*, and *Larry*—your love and nurturing came at a very crucial time in my life so I could quietly move into this work.

Thank you to all my *previous students* who forgave typos, and bad sentence structure, and dead ends in this work. You taught me a lot. A whole lot. Thank you to the brilliant gang at Nova Southeastern University in the Brain-based Teaching and Learning Department: *Dr. Donna Wilson* and *Marcus Conyers* for building an amazing graduate program and *Mary Collington* and for herding grad students. Thank you to all the professors. Lovely work.

Finally, thank you to my dear friends *Tamara Melcher*, *Laura Waldman, Vera Chieffo, and Ann Kennedy* who listened endlessly to my ongoing enthusiasm about this project. And thank you to the gang: *Donna* and *Craig Freiburger*, *Vicki Buch and Jim Pacey, Jim* and *Victoria Cannon*—all the love and laughter has silently supported me for years and years.

INTRODUCTION

As a child, I entered a sublime world of magical creativity in which I made paintings and drawings, carved rocks, and created stories. Looking back, this world was my childhood salvation from a reality marred by poverty, abuse, and neglect. These creative ventures were also a conduit, a portal for accessing profound realms of effortlessness. While I sketched, painted, and wrote, time disappeared. Hours felt like minutes. Gone were the judgmental voices. Harping criticism was nowhere to be found. This effortless world was all mine, christening me as the creative kid. However, years later after extensive life experience and academic research I recognized that this state of effortlessness is much, much larger than our traditional view of creativity. Eventually I came to understand, and now teach, that *anyone* can access this realm of effortlessness, regardless of "creative" abilities.

My first "art" show was held one hot summer afternoon in the backyard of our home in San Antonio, Texas. While the neighborhood kids were busy playing softball or chasing horned toads in the alleys, I proudly sat behind a makeshift table displaying dozens of newly sculpted sandstone shapes carved into rounded, abstract shapes. Only one neighbor boy sauntered into the backyard that sweltering day. His mission: he wanted me to play softball. My mission: I wanted him to buy a sculpture for a nickel. When he realized I would not be swinging a bat, he shrugged his shoulders and scampered away. My only potential customer disappeared before I could give my sales pitch!!

While this first art show was an entrepreneurial disappointment, the experience did not deter me from repeatedly

"... these creative ventures were also a conduit, a portal for accessing profound realms of effortlessness."

entering what felt like divine moments of creativity. I recall losing all sense of time while painting mountain scenes with the next-door neighbors. During a high school art class, I sketched images from art books with a favorite teacher, Mother Murphy. These moments gently opened up a world of timelessness, endless energy, and effortlessness. During the creative process I felt safe, at home, and content. With youthful naiveté, I figured everyone could readily access his or her creative "flow." It would be many years later—well into my 30's while teaching creativity to adult learners—that I humbly learned otherwise.

During my first semester of teaching, I became acutely aware of how difficult it was for most individuals to attain this state of flow, this experience of effortlessness. Many of my students seemed unable to embrace a process that simply *allowed* for the next sketch to occur without premeditated thought. This was the crucial point at which many became stuck. Most of them boldly marched up to that moment only to shrink away, unable to surrender into this flow. As a result of retreating from these powerful moments, students would either miss the deadline or show up with marginal work

For those unable to "let go," this scenario appeared to be universal, regardless of age, ethnicity, or gender. Creativity became an ongoing struggle involving a good deal of sweat—a struggle that ended with procrastination or bouts of debilitating perfectionism. In addition, this pattern triggered considerable amounts of stress while undermining self-confidence.

Students who did succeed in producing novel work were quite unaware as to how they "got to" that work. Their

"... I figured everyone could readily access his or her creative "flow." It would be many years later—well into my 30's while teaching creativity to adult learners—that I humbly learned otherwise."

explanation of the process went something like this: *Well, I just sat down at the table and worked,* or *I had a good creative day,* or *I had my mojo on.* Many students were convinced that some mysterious process was going on over which they had little control. Nothing could have been further from the truth!!

I also recognized that students were not the only ones buying into the concept that "creativity just happens." Many of my family members, friends, and colleagues viewed their own creativity in a similar light, either identifying themselves as creative individuals, or not. Based on decades of experience and observation as an educator, artist, and writer, I now believe that everyone—without exception—has the ability to access his or her own process of creativity: that is, a state of effortlessness. *However, to do so, we must first change our societal concepts that view creativity simply as the output of a "creative" product such as a painting, novel, or song.*

To be in the creative process means partaking of any activity (not just the traditional arts) that allows us to experience *effortlessness, endless energy, and timelessness!* An example comes from a friend who was cleaning out boxes to begin the staging process of selling her home. During her call she excitedly proclaimed, "Linda!! I am in effortlessness cleaning out boxes!" I had to chuckle. I knew once she experienced this delicate flow, it would become difficult for her to ignore an inner urge to return to that flow. However, I can hear some of you. Cleaning out a closet is one thing. Writing a novel is another! Or is it?

For those of you who are writing novels, starting new businesses, or learning how to paint, you may be thinking

"… we must first change our societal concepts that view creativity simply as the output of a 'creative' product such as a painting, novel, or song."

right about now, "Accessing flow is a mystery!" Other readers may be lamenting, "Doesn't it take a lot of effort to experience effortlessness?" Yes, of course, in the beginning, learning any new process to unveil the mystery requires effort—in fact, a lot of effort. However, once a new concept becomes "fired and wired" in the brain, the learner has the opportunity to shift the new skill into a habit. For a writer, simply showing up to the computer on a daily basis becomes more effortless than not—sort of an effortless effort. Developing a clear intent for an endeavor, followed by consistent effort, paves the way to experience the pinnacle of the process of creativity: effortlessness.

People often tell me that life gets in the way of doing what they want to do—whether it be writing a children's book, creating a web series, or planting a garden. This sounds like, "I'm too busy with my job/my spouse/the kids/my boyfriend or girlfriend." Of course, life happens and real challenges do exist around time, money, and energy. But oftentimes we blame external events, situations, or people to hide our lack of self-confidence. My personal favorite came from the vice president of a rather large firm: "I don't have the confidence to publish my writing." (I might add that his writing was an inspirational joy to read!) How could the vice president of a multimillion dollar enterprise make such a statement?

Regardless of our positions in life, many of us harbor the following pesky thought: I can't do this or that because of my struggle with x, y, or z. It does not matter if we are rich or poor, young or old; why don't we try a couple of new thoughts? Rather than focusing on the struggle with x, y, or z, how about applying

"Regardless of our positions in life, many of us harbor the following pesky thought: I can't do this or that because of my struggle with x, y, or z."

the efforts of a, b, and c *instead*? Based on years of teaching experience and graduate work in brain-based teaching and learning—coupled with life-transforming travels to Nepal and India—I have developed strategies for assisting others to access their state of effortlessness, regardless of life situation!

In summary, no matter the level of your creative abilities or your specific life situation, you can learn how to apply and practice the process of creativity with any endeavor. Most important, through this process, you can begin to experience the state of effortlessness or, as I prefer to call it—Thuse. Through continued practice you extend effortlessness into your daily life, moving beyond struggle, beyond reactive natures. With Thuse, you can become a little lightbulb of enthusiasm, seemingly sprinkled with magical pixie dust. At some point, with Thuse you could shift into the Mind of Thuse—an unquantifiable, amorphous space that just knows what it knows without thinking. *Thriving within effortlessness, and within the Mind of Thuse,* is real and is yours for the taking.

"Most importantly, through this process, you can experience the state of effortlessness or, as I prefer to call it—Thuse."

1

MY
story

Creativity was a process that led me back to effortlessness and timelessness. At the time, I had no idea that I could overlay this creative flow of effortlessness onto all aspects of my life.

CHAPTER ONE

MY STORY

As a Catholic schoolgirl growing up in San Antonio, Texas, I recall being interrupted from my ABC's one afternoon and hurriedly ushered into the school church sanctuary. Lined up in rows of pews were nuns, all kneeling, with heads hanging over their rosaries— and desperately praying. President Kennedy had just been shot. The air was stagnant with shock, thick with fear. We recited Hail Mary after Hail Mary, begging for John Kennedy's life. At 1:00 p.m. our Catholic hero and president was pronounced dead. It seemed the lifelike statues of Mary and Joseph could have crumbled from the weight of grief.

"The following months and years may be summed up in one word—tumultuous."

Around this same time, another incident occurred to shake my small world. My father disappeared. He left home and never looked back to his wife and four children. Overnight we became the only single-parent family on the block. Not a word was uttered as to why he left. The following months and years may be summed up in one word—tumultuous. No phone calls were forthcoming from my father. No birthday cards. No letters. Not even a single postcard. Nothing. Later I discovered he had never sent one penny of child support.

Because my mother had birthed four babies in the short time of five years, her body had ballooned into severe obesity. With my father gone, her grief transpired into inconsolable depression. To numb the pain, she continued to eat and to read books—countless books to feed her highly intelligent mind. She did this while lying in bed for hours and hours. As the oldest child, I assumed many of her neglected adult responsibilities. This included daily chores, such as cleaning the living room, dining room, and kitchen areas—including, of course, the dreaded pile of dirty dishes. With money being tight, around age nine or ten, I convinced my mother to allow me to be the caretaker of my younger siblings. She agreed. These increased responsibilities came with no motherly hugs, very little encouragement, and no I love you's. My mom may have read a dozen books during the week, but reading a bedtime story to her kids was not in the cards. Although my mother loved her children dearly, she simply could not take care of them.

"... creativity cradled me in a world of magical imagination. This creativity carried me into a place of effortlessness and timelessness ..."

Without my father's income, our family struggled with basic bills, including food and clothing. Although my mother had a college degree and a decent job, a pot of beans became the family staple. Spam, potpies, and six hamburgers for a dollar served as our means of sustenance. Yet, in spite of the extra responsibilities and worries, everything seemed balanced—though precariously. But then came the worst, which occurred the summer after I took charge of my siblings. With mother at work, my sisters and I were left alone in the house. We were an unprotected group of three preteen girls: a highway billboard for trouble. Teenage boys intruded, took advantage, and marred us into unspoken codes of silence. My brain took a nosedive. The delicate balance now tipped, leaving me in a dark abyss that resulted in memory lapse. To this day, I am unable to recall the names of my fifth and sixth grade teachers.

However, a sweet little light remained tucked away in the corner of my mind. Throughout the whole of childhood, creativity cradled me in a world of magical imagination. This creativity carried me into a place of effortlessness and timelessness; I sketched everything, from notebook covers depicting flying airplanes to portraits of well-known cartoon characters. My mother, also a writer and creative being, *always* encouraged my creative nature.

During seventh grade, Sister Ann, a young Irish nun, took an interest in me. I loved Sister Ann dearly. She simply knew how to love. I can still feel her protective presence quietly standing in the background. Her loving concern, coupled with my artistic creativity, slowly guided me out of the darkness of those fifth- and sixth-grade years. Nevertheless, the scars, although invisible, now acted as subconscious demons and wedged side by side with my creativity. Sister Ann could not follow me to the new public school I attended but her love remained and strengthened me.

LIVING ON THE EDGE OF STRUGGLE

As an insecure teen, I learned how to quietly steal away to draw or paint. In the evenings, painting with an older couple across the street became my oasis. At first, they showed me how to paint by numbers. In a matter of days, I was painting originals. Creativity had become my savior. Yet little did I know that my escape into creativity was also a split from reality. Life as I knew it was too painful. My brain had to find an escape to survive, cope, and adapt the pain of unacknowledged childhood trauma. Repairing the split would become a lifelong endeavor.

Graduating from high school and moving into a college dorm brought a certain amount of freedom. I decided to major in commercial art, a means of using art to build a career. By the second year—not realizing I had to reapply for loans and grants—university life became a financial struggle. To pay my bills, I began working the evening shift as a full-time waitress in a truck stop.

"... My brain had to find an escape to cope, adapt, and survive the pain of unacknowledged childhood trauma. Repairing the split would become a lifelong endeavor."

Twenty dollars in tips each night became my cash cow. Forget about sleep. I could maintain a full class schedule during the day and work until 2:00 a.m. Struggle was becoming deeply embedded, not only as a learned habit but also as an acceptable way to live. The split in my life widened, between experiencing effortlessness through creativity and simply struggling to survive.

Once out of college, the struggle continued. During my first job, I often worked 60 hours a week even when overtime was not needed or expected. At age 23, I married and was separated within 11 months. After the divorce I juggled three "committed" relationships. Yes, struggle was here to stay and remained a familiar yet undesirable companion. From this dysfunctional point of view, I had to work really, really hard to accomplish anything.

In contrast, creativity was a process that led me back to effortlessness and timelessness. At the time, I had no idea that I could overlay this creative flow of effortlessness onto all aspects of my life. What a mental disconnect! My established behavioral pattern—struggle, struggle, struggle—was in charge and directing my life. With this much angst, I developed a wide range of addictions. At the height of my addictive phase, I was smoking a pack or two of cigarettes while painting in the evenings. The best poetry I ever wrote came on the heels of a drunken episode. My weight was a yo-yo from my being a compulsive overeater. No money? No problem. I would write a string of bounced checks each month that cost at least $200 in fees.

Relationships entered and exited through a revolving door; three months was about all I could handle. Exercise? Sure. I trained for four marathons while ignoring the fact that my body was

"Yes, struggle was here to stay and remained a familiar yet undesirable companion. From this dysfunctional point of view, I had to work really, really hard to accomplish anything."

physically hurt. Even as an artist—a freelance graphic designer—I constantly worried about finding the next project to pay my rent. I was a mess. Yet deep down inside I wanted to stop this insanity.

Finally, following a string of bizarre incidents that resulted in locating my father, a friend convinced me to get professional help. Thus, beginning in my mid-twenties, a group of wonderfully talented therapists, spiritual teachers, and friends came forward and helped to open, as well as heal, my world. For the next two decades, I kicked, screamed, shook, got angry, and cried. It took years to uncover the trauma of my earliest body memories of an ongoing and unwanted inappropriate touch from my father. I now know why the Catholic priest told my mother to divorce my father. Priests did not give such advice in the early 1960's. But eventually, I healed. Life changed dramatically as my brain, heart, and soul gradually relinquished identification with struggle.

"… eventually, I healed. Life changed dramatically as my brain, heart, and soul gradually relinquished identification with struggle."

THE TREK OF A LIFETIME

At the age of 41, I made a Himalayan trek to base camp Mount Everest. On the second day of this adventure, I hiked up a mountain for eight hours, a trek punctuated by exhausting effort and struggle. By the time we reached our destination, I had developed full-blown altitude sickness. A very observant lodge owner noticed my state of confusion and probed me with a few questions. Within a minute, she turned to my guide Dawa and demanded: "Take her down off the mountain, NOW!" Even in my stupor I knew the sunlight was waning. Yet the closest lodge was two hours down the challenging path that we had just ascended. I begged to be rescued by helicopter.

During the next ten minutes, life became a blur. Dawa repacked my duffle bag and had us literally running back down the extremely rocky trail. The cliffs on my right were sheer thousand foot drop-offs. Even though I held a walking stick in my right hand for balance and Dawa firmly held my left hand, altitude sickness had fogged my brain and feet. I stumbled, tripped, and slid. Unbeknownst to me, something mysterious was quietly happening. You see, this trip was not just a midlife adventure to reach base camp Mount Everest. I had known intuitively that this journey was going to reveal something profound to me.

"… this trip was not just a midlife adventure to reach base camp Mount Everest. I had known intuitively that this journey was going to reveal something profound to me."

As a young girl I had cultivated a deeply spiritual side, first with Catholicism and later in my twenties with the study of Hinduism and Buddhism. In my life experience the spiritual and the creative had mirrored each other. Both meditation and creativity had allowed me to experience a deep peace, very much like the joyous calm of effortlessness. As a result, I traveled to India with the intention of learning how to practice internal quiet. Yet, despite my experience in India, the split remained between the ongoing need to struggle and the undeniable experience of effortlessness that I felt in spiritual and creative sessions. Unfortunately, struggle was winning and still running the show.

Now in the Himalayas, fuzzy with altitude sickness, running down a rocky path while slipping and sliding as darkness descended, something had to give. Struggle HAD to give way to effortlessness. If not, the consequences would prove disastrous. While silently focusing on effortlessness by repeating a meditative phrase, my mind and body started to calm. Within a few minutes I quit stumbling. Somehow my footsteps began to land in the right place again and again. For the next hour and a half—and now in the dark—my stumbling completely stopped. I was nimble footed, effortlessly running down the mountain feeling buoyant and light. How had this happened?

Once back in the States something equally peculiar occurred. My outlook on life dramatically shifted from struggle to more ease and effortlessness. My career changed. As a result, money started flowing abundantly. I was able to buy a home, able to take care of an old tax debt. My spiritual life deepened. More than anything, I started to trust and become quiet enough to hear the internal direction that guided me. The split was healing.

From the experience on the mountain, I learned firsthand that the flow of effortlessness is not just inherent in the process of creativity and meditation but in all aspects of life. Today, I simply have to recognize when I'm not aligned with my effortless state and then take the necessary steps to reestablish my state of balance. Now, of course, this has taken practice—a lot of practice combined with a deep acknowledgment and healing of a troubled childhood. The payoff, however, has been huge and explains why I am forever a student of the powerful state of effortlessness—Thuse.

"From the experience on the mountain, I learned firsthand that the flow of effortlessness is not just inherent in the process of creativity and meditation but in all aspects of life."

2

THE
process of creativity

*People are the most alive, most vibrant, and most content when
they can readily access their process of creativity leading to
effortlessness on a regular basis—regardless of the specific activity.*

CHAPTER TWO

WE LOVE DISCOVERING SOMETHING NEW

To those who experience life as struggle, hard work, and constant effort, the concept of effortlessness may seem incomprehensible. But is it really? Stop and think about a time when you could work on a project for hours. Perhaps you were fixing a car, baking a cake, or creating a make-believe story for a child. Did you lose track of time? Did you forget that you were hungry? You may have been experiencing the flow of effortlessness. The experience of effortlessness is for everyone, including those holding fast to the idea that this sort of flow belongs only to "creative" people.

In *Creativity: Flow and the Psychology of Discovery and Invention*, author Mihalyi Csikszentmihalyi asked people to describe what they most enjoyed doing. Regardless of the specific act, a frequent response was "designing or discovering something new" (Csikszentmihalyi, 1996). Indeed, throughout our lives, we are in the process of creating or discovering something new. Let's take this concept even further.

We may say that an artist is creative when s/he picks up a paintbrush and decides to dab it into yellow, then strokes that color onto a canvas. Now imagine this same artist rather than making discrete decisions to paint certain strokes instead becomes a conduit for creativity by stroking paint across the canvas without a preconceived notion or thought. When the artist is in the flow of this process of creativity, the painting seems to paint itself. This flow within the process of creativity leads us into effortlessness—into Thuse. Further, it is this effortless creativity that cannot be "controlled" and may, as a result, be

"The experience of effortlessness is for everyone, including those holding fast to the idea that this sort of flow belongs only to 'creative' people."

considered a tad uncomfortable for those more accustomed to a linear, logical sequence.

Once we start to understand that, instead of a painter painting the painting, the painting begins to paint itself then we have to understand the role of the painter. Now it may seem that the painter is a facilitator but in actuality, when within the flow of the process of creativity, s/he is an observer. Understanding that actuality is when life shifts—and I mean a profound shift.

"We think this experience is fleeting and only for profound moments. We are wrong."

As I delve deeper into research, I am coming to acknowledge that *few understand the process of creativity. We think this experience is fleeting and only for profound moments. We are wrong.* Some of you will instantly understand the above and are simply ready to bring the process of creativity more fully into your lives. Others may want and need a more detailed explanation.

Individuals who have experienced firsthand the process of creativity leading into effortlessness refer to it as *the zone, the sweet spot* or, as one of my students called it, *gettin' my groove on.* Most people imagine this as a fleeting experience, reserved only for highly creative individuals and then only for rare and special moments. What if I were to tell you that this deeply fulfilling experience is not as mysterious as you think and may be easily learned, understood, and utilized in day-to-day life? Yep. Clap on. Clap off. Turn effortlessness on. Turn effortlessness off.

Consider the following statement: the phenomenon leading to *effortlessness* is what I describe as the *process* of creativity and not creativity itself. For instance, Leonardo da Vinci is considered a consummately creative individual for painting the Mona Lisa (among other things). But it was more than likely his *process* of creativity—becoming lost in the act—that allowed for that masterpiece to come forth. When coming down the mountain, my struggle had to give way to an effortlessness that I had previously experienced only while painting or drawing. *Effortlessly running down that mountain— placing one foot in the exact right spot again and again—in spite of a rocky trail, darkness, and altitude sickness—became equivalent to my brushstrokes effortlessly sweeping across a canvas!* I now fully believe that we are supposed to live each and every moment of our lives in this exact effortless state. That's a big statement—I know … but let's go even a little further out on a limb to explore the process of creativity.

Each of us is unique. Each of us engages in unique endeavors. These endeavors are like "vehicles" in that we use them to enter the process of creativity. Currently, my vehicle is writing; in the past, they have also been painting, designing, and illustrating. When beginning to consider undertaking an endeavor, imagine it as a vehicle parked in your driveway. That vehicle can't get anywhere without a little gas and a road that leads to a final destination. If you're caught up in struggle, your vehicle is broken down. But with effort, you'll pull out of the driveway onto the road of the process of creativity. Cruising that road eventually takes you to the Land of Thuse, your state of effortlessness. Of course, there is much more to the process but this illustrates the bare bones of how you reach effortlessness.

Now, I'm no da Vinci, but I enjoy developing something new that is uniquely engaging to me—just like da Vinci! My

"When beginning to consider undertaking an endeavor, imagine it as a vehicle parked in your driveway. That vehicle can't get anywhere without a little gas and a road that leads to a final destination."

11

process, your process, da Vinci's process of creativity is one and the same. Our vehicles are just different.

For example, your vehicle may be a love of baking. Cakes, cookies, bread, and pastries—no one leaves your home empty-handed. That love of baking may lead you to quit your job and open a bakery. What happens when the joy of baking does not translate to understanding accounting, working with people, or getting up at 3:00 in the morning? Effortlessness flies out the window! That is why understanding the process of creativity *while baking* will open the door to more effortlessness when operating other aspects of your bakery business. This is how we begin to live effortlessness within each moment of our lives. *From years of observation, research, and experience, I have determined that people are the most alive, most vibrant, and most content when they can readily access their process of creativity leading to effortlessness on a regular basis—regardless of the specific activity.* Currently, my inner process of creativity also shows up when I'm building websites, designing video, teaching a class, or figuring out how to solve open code problems.

Now ... what happens when one perceives his/her unique vehicle as dormant or inaccessible? Actually, your vehicle *wants* to come out of that driveway. How many times have you thought the following: "If only I had this or that, *then* I could do what I really want!" The very nature of our humanness tends to block access to aligning with what we really want for ourselves. By "humanness," I mean that wide spectrum of human emotions and struggles, such as feeling frustrated and stressed while working on a challenging math problem or feeling fearful when dealing

"... I have determined that people are the most alive, most vibrant, and most content when they can readily access their process of creativity leading to effortlessness on a regular basis—regardless of the specific activity."

with a costly car repair (especially with limited resources in the bank). That humanness will keep us so busy with the struggle of solving daily problems that we have no energy, no gas left to pull our vehicle out of the driveway and start traveling!!

Learning to trust the subtle force of effortlessness feels unfamiliar and, therefore, challenging. In fact, most of us have grown from children to adults completely unaware of the inherent state of effortlessness. Most of us are accustomed to reacting from the humanness of learned struggle and, as a result, more often than not experience feelings of being overwhelmed, frustration, and fear. Deeply ingrained habits based on upbringing, education, and culture paint a picture that legitimizes struggle. Think about a recent event that challenged you to the core. Did you place most of your attention on struggle? Aligning with effortlessness becomes next to impossible when you're tied up in knots with stress, angst, or worry.

Nevertheless, we all get tiny glimpses of effortlessness, like a young child playing hide-and-seek. In one moment we see our effortlessness; the next moment it disappears. Yet if we look closely enough, we are provided a wonderful set of clues that are like a road map to the Land of Thuse. How, you might ask?

First, *acknowledge* that your vehicle is sitting in the driveway, revving up to get your attention. What endeavor, project, or activity have you been ruminating on, without taking action? Then, try to put aside your humanness—even for five minutes. Try to think beyond those thoughts of humanness that keep you from doing what you want to do.

"… acknowledge that your vehicle is sitting in the driveway, revving up to get your attention. What endeavor, project, or activity have you been ruminating on, without taking action?"

Next, flirt with your activity. If you've been having an urge to paint, pick up the paintbrush and hold it. Open a cookbook and read a new recipe. Write the first sentence that comes to your mind. Research the costs of a video camera. Afterwards, make note of your experience. Hints of effortlessness from these small tasks may awaken an inner urge to explore your process of creativity. As we pay careful attention to these moments, we learn how to further cultivate and sustain our process of creativity leading to the state of effortlessness.

Once you have some understanding of effortlessness, with practice, the process of creativity starts to become a regular part of your life. In time, effortlessness may also be applied to areas that are highly challenging to many of us such as dealing with a difficult co-worker, writing a lengthy term paper for school, or completing your taxes. This list is, of course, endless. As we learn to thrive within effortlessness, we become more able to solve a variety of problems, whether simple or complex. So once again, why don't we live in this delightful manner all the time?

When coming down off that mountain in the Himalayas, putting one foot in front of the other, I entered into an extraordinary state of effortlessness, much to my astonishment. Now, mind you, it has taken years of effort to sort out what actually happened on that mountain and more years still to develop, become familiar with, and practice my own state of effortlessness. However, the result is that I have a much calmer, less fearful demeanor. Of course, being fully human, I still get blindsided and forget my effortlessness. But because I am an

"In time, effortlessness may also be applied to highly challenging areas such as dealing with a difficult co-worker, writing a lengthy term paper for school, or completing your taxes. This list is, of course, endless."

ardent student of this process, my practice allows me to quickly recognize and then halt struggle. Within minutes I realign with effortlessness. Practice, it takes practice!!

Yes, learning how to apply the process of creativity takes work. My students often remind me of this fact in the early learning stages. But, it gets easier—with practice. One of the benefits of this practice is a sublime and constant state of discovery, leading us into spaces that we, in our humanness, never imagined possible. At this point, why not take a moment to recognize some of your own moments of effortlessness? If none come to mind, that is totally fine. For those who do recall such experiences, here's a question: why are such moments of effortlessness fleeting?

FLOW BABY FLOW

In 1990, Csikszentmihalyi described a state of mind he called flow: "... the individual experiences intense satisfaction, losing all sense of time, place, and extraneous physical sensations. In such a state, the individual is so absorbed in the event that nothing else intrudes into awareness" (Csikszentmihalyi, 1990). Furthermore, in an interview with *Wired Magazine*, Csikszentmihalyi referred to flow as "being completely involved in an activity for its own sake. The ego falls away. Time flies. Every action, movement, and thought follows inevitably from the *previous* one, like playing jazz. Your whole being is involved, and you're using your skills to the utmost" (Geirland, 2004). Csikszentmihalyi's research and analysis is quite similar to what we have been discussing. Now that we're acquainted with the concept of flow let's explore how

"... it gets easier—with practice. One of the benefits of this practice is a sublime and constant state of discovery, leading us into spaces that we, in our humanness, never imagined possible."

15

to *consciously* tap into this flow when faced with daily challenges, such as solving math problems or paying monthly bills or dealing with car repair.

JANE'S CAR BREAKS DOWN

When we perceive a problem as unsolvable, effortlessness goes by the wayside. We may become frustrated, irritated. We may worry, become angry, or just give up. How might we address problems differently if effortlessness is *integrated* into our lives? To proceed, we need to imagine two characters that decide whether or not we can slip into effortlessness. One character is a "good cop." The other is a "bad cop." How would you react if your car broke down and funds in the bank were already stretched?

"How might we address problems differently if effortlessness is integrated into our lives? To proceed, we need to imagine two characters that decide whether or not we can slip into effortlessness."

Recently my friend Jane was stuck in the middle of a grocery store parking lot unable to start her car. Wanting to help, I agreed to pick her up and drive her home. When I arrived on the scene, it appeared to me that all was fine because the tow was in progress. However, upon approaching her, I realized that Jane's "bad cop" was front and center. Stress was doing quite a number on her. With only $40 in her bank account, she was in a panic about the upcoming repair. I gently reminded her of the benefits of staying calm and temporarily setting fear aside. However, Jane's stress had already fogged her thinking; she wasn't even able to decide on a repair shop. After a couple of calls and suggestions from others, however, she finally decided where to have the car towed.

The next day, the repair shop called with a quote of $850. Again, as she was about to fall into a panic, she "heard" me say

once again: "Calm down. Effortlessness is at your fingertips."
After hanging up the phone, Jane's "good cop" finally stepped
forward. At this pivotal and important point, Jane clearly began
to observe her own struggle. It was then she made a conscious
choice to sit quietly and calm herself. With a few key questions
(that we'll address in a later chapter), Jane uncovered why she was
struggling. As a result, Jane's ability to step back and "observe" her
own behavior helped to soothe her stressed brain. She just needed
to be nudged and reminded that effortlessness was possible, even
when faced with costly car repair.

    Jane accepted that, although an immediate answer was
not available, a second opinion would be best. Perhaps another
repair shop would be less expensive. It is important to note that
my friend made a conscious choice to access the quiet in her
brain to problem solve at that particular moment. By quieting
her thoughts, Jane's humanness began to calm. As a result, she
was able to align with effortlessness. This process of calming
and aligning allowed her to recall the name of a reputable yet
inexpensive auto tech. In fact, while this guy repaired Jane's car,
she was offered the use of a friend's car for the entire week.

    A few days later, the repair was completed for $260,
as opposed to $850. As Jane continued to align with her
effortlessness, more of her problems were solved. For instance,
out of the clear blue, a couple of small jobs cropped up
unexpectedly, earning Jane an additional $220. By the time
the repair was complete, Jane handed over $260 in cash to the
mechanic. Jane's ability to curb stress allowed her to tap into the
"good cop" (becoming and remaining calm) while avoiding the

"It is important to note that my friend made a conscious choice to access the quiet in her brain to problem solve at that particular moment."

"bad cop" (falling into a fear-based mental fog) that would have sabotaged creative problem solving. Perhaps if she had remained calm initially, Jane might have remembered the name of the second repair shop while sitting in the parking lot—and saved herself a good deal of upset. Regardless, Jane ultimately slipped into a mind set of contemplation and equanimity that allowed her to arrive at the solution. Furthermore, she was able to "trust the process" to such a degree that unexpected opportunities arose for her to earn additional funds.

We can all identify with my friend's dilemma because who doesn't face daily stressful incidents, both large and small? Too much stress, or the inability to manage stress, causes struggle and thwarts our ability to operate within effortlessness. Now let's take a closer look at some of those behind-the-scenes culprits that block our paths to effortlessness.

3

stress in the 'hood

Simply acknowledging that you are stressed, admitting that you do
not have an immediate answer, yet trusting that you will be guided to
an answer will often take the edge off and reduce anxiety.

CHAPTER THREE

NO MORE STRESS PLEASE!

Stress. Let's face it—our fast-paced society is somewhat addicted to this "bad cop" running rampant in our 'hoods. Although stress has proven time and again to wreak havoc on our mental and physical states, the sneaky culprit has established itself as an acceptable way of life. That's a problem. Ongoing stress deeply entrenches each of us in the belief that struggle is necessary to survive. And, although we don't really want to acknowledge this dirty little secret of daily and ongoing stress, deep down inside, we know there's truth to the tale.

In the seventh century, the Buddhist monk Seng-Ts'an wrote the following: "The Great Way is not difficult for those who have no preferences" (Seng-ts'an, n.d.). Yes, I will be the first to admit that having no preferences is a tall, tall order for our humanness to swallow. Nevertheless, let's take a look at what he's attempting to say by addressing the "bad cop" of stress. What causes us the most stress?

At the most basic level, ingrained survival mechanisms left over from the days of the dinosaurs still actively protect us. Although the dangers are long gone, instead of worrying about Tyrannosaurus rex lurking around the bend, we fear for the safety of our family, friends, homes, children, pets, finances, and health. Let's face it: we like what we like. We have a preference to keep all of our cherished treasures safe and sound.

But wouldn't a problem arise—much like the menace of a dinosaur—if a danger threatened to hurt one of our loved ones, places, or things? And what if we were unable to solve this problem by removing the threat? Furthermore, what if

"... although we don't really want to acknowledge this dirty little secret of daily and ongoing stress, deep down inside, we know there's truth to the tale."

our perception of the danger was much greater than the actual danger? Would a perceived threat cause us as much stress as that of a real threat?

In modern society, high stress levels occur when we *perceive* that we cannot quickly fix a problem that is right in front of us. Why? For starters, each one of us is a unique blend of likes and dislikes. We tend to align with others who hold similar beliefs. In this way, we form bonds through friendships, marriages, communities, religions, and countries. To protect such bonds, the brain insists that we staunchly stand by our embedded preferences that then form our deeply ingrained beliefs. At times circumstances arise in which we perceive an inability to protect these kinships.

But for just a minute, let's pretend that we had no such bonds. How would we be affected if we had no perceptions, beliefs, or preferences? For most, this simple exercise jolts the brain into an uncomfortable tilt. Why? Herein lies the culprit. Our brains are giant storehouses of beliefs, emotions, memories, perceptions, and preferences that, in turn, form habits. Because most of us overidentify with our preferences, beliefs, and habits, any threat to the status quo can easily stir up fear—fear of losing our identity or losing someone dear to us, or losing something precious and valuable, or someplace familiar and safe. Who wants to lose what we like?

One of my favorite companions is Spiff, my little Siamese cat. Everyday, while she snuggles and purrs in delight, I profusely thank the cosmos for my Spiff. My preferences have formed habits: she lies in my lap while I write, sleeps under the

"For most, this simple exercise jolts the brain into an uncomfortable tilt. Why? Herein lies the culprit. Our brains are giant storehouses of beliefs, emotions, memories, perceptions, and preferences that, in turn, form habits."

covers at night, and sits out in the morning sun while I drink coffee (alright, alright, I am a cat lady). My bond with Spiff is so strong that if I am not careful with my thoughts, within a short few minutes I become sad, teary-eyed, and *stressed* just thinking about the potential loss of my friend. Yes, someday she will be gone. But heck, right now, she's in my arms!! I have formed a preference for my little cat to always be around. Now ... that's simply not going to happen.

But because of my preference, I will often "make up" a scenario in which Spiff becomes sick. As a result of this scenario, I begin to experience a perceived loss (which is actually not true in the moment). This potential loss leads to the development of a problem that I perceive is unsolvable (again, the problem does not currently exist). Being unable to solve the problem causes stress—even though the problem may be in the future! All of this jibber jabber internal dialogue is quite unnecessary, yet we all do it. We allow our minds to create perceived threats that do not exist—and then stress out because we think we're about to lose something!

What else causes us more grief, tears, and anguish than loss? Whether through perception (which may be imagined) or through actually losing a loved one, home, marriage, friend, or job, deep down inside we may harbor expectations that somehow we should have been able to avoid that loss. We should have been better at solving that particular problem! If only we could have found a cure for the illness, or come up with enough money to pay the mortgage, or identified the right therapist to salvage our

"All of this jibber jabber internal dialogue is quite unnecessary, yet we all do it. We allow our minds to create perceived threats that do not exist ..."

marriage. Being unable to find a solution makes us feel helpless and out of control, and quite *stressed.*

Real losses are indeed devastating—and deserve to be acknowledged and grieved. However, these losses are only half the problem. Ready for the second half? It is not only the unsolvable problem that causes stress but also the unacknowledged, yet perceived, fear of *losing some aspect of one's self* that causes stress. To further illustrate, let's return to Jane and her car.

The glaringly obvious reason for Jane's stress was her *perception* that she could not solve the problem by fixing her car with only $40. Her humanness of panic was at a loss for a solution and thus, a secondary, yet quite unacknowledged, thought arose: she might lose her car. But that thought was just half of the problem. The other half lay deeply hidden within her brain.

Digging deeper—without a car, Jane's freedom to move around the city would be significantly limited—hence, she would lose her freedom of mobility. The real culprit of her stress was not just a "broken-down" car, but rather her subconscious fear of losing a cherished aspect of herself: independence. *Fear of losing some aspect of our identity becomes the real but hidden mob boss activating the obvious "bad cop" of stress.*

Recurring thoughts of potential loss—such as Jane's fear of losing mobility and freedom—become subconscious and super-sneaky culprits that continually feed our stress! Just the anxious thought, conscious or not, that we are going to "lose something" produces immediate stress.

"The real culprit of her stress was not just a 'broken-down' car, but rather her subconscious fear of losing a cherished aspect of herself: independence."

This is the primary reason for being unable to live in effortlessness. The threat of having one more thing or person taken away from us lies just below the conscious surface, waiting for the next stressful trigger. At this point, you may say, "Well isn't that just life?" Sure. But let's take a closer look at what goes on in the body, and in the brain specifically, before we accept a life of daily stress.

THE POWERFUL BRAIN TIMES THREE

We know that the brain is a powerful tool. Brilliant brains have conceived amazing theories and mechanisms—from string theory to the Hubble telescope viewing the birth of stars. Yes ... all quite fascinating. The two brain hemispheres—left and right—are covered by a cortex, which is composed of six layers of rich cells about 1/10th of an inch thick (Sousa, 2006). Even though the size of the cortex is that of a dinner napkin, the cells can expand into "10,000 miles of connecting fibers per cubic inch" (Sousa, 2006, p. 20). That is a *lot* of thinking power. But these supersmarts did not happen overnight.

Over millions of years, the brain evolved in three distinct stages of development: the reptilian brain, the midbrain, and the cerebral cortex. Each brain has its own set of individual functions, yet they must all work harmoniously together to champion the process of creativity leading us into an effortless state. Shall we turn to biology and explore the first brain?

"Over millions of years, the brain evolved in three distinct stages of development: the reptilian brain, the midbrain, and the cerebral cortex."

THE FIRST BRAIN: THE LIZARD BRAIN

The first and most basic part of the brain, the *reptilian* or *lizard brain*—also referred to as the *brain stem*—evolved 500 million years ago during the Paleozoic era. This brain is simple, "geared only to the maintenance of survival functions such as respiration, circulation, and reproduction" (Howard, 2006, p. 45). We breathe. We have blood coursing through our veins. We have babies. That's the function of the reptilian brain—to operate autonomously and behind the scenes, akin to a computer operating system.

"Functioning from the survival brain causes snap judgments and involuntary responses to problems based on instinct, habits, and routine behavior."

With Jane's initial thought of losing her car, the lizard brain kicked in and triggered an instantaneous, automatic reaction of fear. Much like being startled and letting out a scream when someone spooks you from behind, Jane reacted with instant panic. As other parts of the brain and central nervous system got involved, her breathing probably shortened and then quickened. Further, the blood moved away from her brain to prime her legs for a quick getaway.

Functioning from the survival brain causes snap judgments and involuntary responses to problems based on instincts, habits, and routine behaviors. Sometimes these reactions are in our best interest, and sometimes they're not. Lucky for us, over the next few million years, a second brain evolved.

THE LEOPARD BRAIN, THE MIDBRAIN, OR THE LIMBIC SYSTEM

The second brain is the *leopard brain*, the *midbrain*, or the *limbic system*. This portion of the brain is responsible for "the generation of emotion and processing of emotional memories" (Sousa, 2006, p. 18). Therefore this brain is also called the *chemical brain* or the *emotional brain*. In addition, this part of the brain houses the limbic system, which interconnects different areas for the "interplay of emotion and reason" such as: 1) the thalamus, 2) the hypothalamus, 3) the hippocampus, and 4) the amygdala (Sousa, 2006, p. 18). Now, you may ask, why should we even care about aspects of the brain? We're long past that biology course. Well … actually there are a few things they didn't tell us in biology class.

The brain is a powerful and complex recording device capable of storing innumerable bits of information. This storage capability allows us to recall facts, emotions, incidents, people, places, and things. How might this influence those of us learning the process of creativity? Without awareness of how the brain uses this information, we can all easily become mere puppets, manipulated by this powerful organ. For instance, imagine you experience something scary, such as watching a friend almost get hit by a car. The factual information of the situation—where the event occurred, the color of car, and the sound of the brakes screeching—is housed (as mentioned earlier) in the cerebral cortex. Yet the amygdala is where the memory of that fear is stored. Two weeks later the sound of screeching brakes will trigger that stored memory—and a fearful response. Your hands will sweat. Your heart will race. Your breath will shorten. But, in reality, no danger exists in the present situation. The car just stopped suddenly to avoid running a red light. Nevertheless, though the facts are not the same, your emotional memory causes

"… you may ask, why should we even care about aspects of the brain? We're long past that biology course. Well … actually there are a few things they didn't tell us in biology class."

you to experience the same fear reaction. So that leads to a very basic question: who's in charge?

When one is feeling sad, anxious, afraid, etc., stored emotional memories are triggering complex, integrated processes and signals within the brain. These processes are varied, ranging from neurotransmitters affecting one's specific emotions to hormone levels interacting with the body (Howard, 2006). In short, these intricate processes may be compared to "chemical dumps" within the brain. For example: two weeks after the above incident, screeching brakes in the present situation triggered a stored emotional memory which then signaled a chemical dump of the fear response. But here is the interesting twist. The stored emotional memory was a perception that had developed from the previous situation. In essence, perceptions, and not necessarily reality, are the mechanism that triggers the brain's chemical dump and subsequent emotional response.

Consider the following: Joseph LeDoux, PhD, professor of psychology and neuroscience at New York University, has stated, "Memories about emotions are just facts" (LeDoux, 1997, August). From a scientific perspective, LeDoux is correct. Emotional memories *ought* to be just facts given that the brain is such a remarkable recording device. But from a psychological and cognitive perspective, the way the brain stores and recalls these memories is not as neutral as the word "facts" suggests. Indeed, these processes often govern present behaviors, undermining our well-being. So the question now is: how does one not only take charge of the brain, but how does one make emotional memories just fact?

"... from a psychological and cognitive perspective, the way the brain stores and recalls these memories is not as neutral as the word 'facts' suggests."

Perhaps during moments of emotional stress, we could remember that the brain is like a computer hard drive of stored information. In this manner, we may then rather observe our emotions objectively rather than be governed by them. I am in no way suggesting that we try to avoid emotional response. Nope, I'm all for keeping our emotions fully intact and allowing them to flow without hindrance. However, while we are experiencing emotions, we need to be aware that they are the result of a temporary chemical output. From this perspective, how might Jane have reacted differently to her car dilemma?

As Jane sat in that parking lot frozen by fear, she felt a perceived threat to her long-held beliefs about freedom. Jane perceived that it would be difficult to get to the grocery store, to her job, to do all those things that need to be done in order to survive. These thoughts were a stressful response that triggered a host of unwanted chemicals and emotions. Yet, with recognition and a few steps, Jane could have quickly offset the effects of the stress.

First, she would have needed to recognize the brain's primary push for survival. Instead of focusing on not having enough money, her awareness could have shifted to the following question: "Do I feel threatened?" Her next thoughts might have been, "Am I breathing deeply and consistently?" "How do I quiet these chattering thoughts?" And then: "I do not have the answer at this moment but that's okay. I don't need to panic." Simply acknowledging that you are stressed, admitting that you do not have an immediate answer, yet trusting that you will be guided to an answer will often take the edge off and reduce anxiety.

"Simply acknowledging that you are stressed, admitting that you do not have an immediate answer, yet trusting that you will be guided to an answer will often take the edge off and reduce anxiety."

While these observations and responses seem quite basic, applying them consciously to each and every stressful incident takes practice. As our self-awareness learns to catch the culprit of survival trying to snare us into stress, reactions to seemingly unsolvable problems become less anxiety driven and more relaxed.

"The cerebral cortex allows us to solve problems, use language and numbers, develop memory, and exercise creativity."

THE THIRD BRAIN: THE CEREBRAL CORTEX

If Jane had remained calm, her thinking would have operated from the third and final brain, the *cerebral cortex.* This outer layer of the brain's most dominant area (the cerebrum) is sometimes referred to as the *creative learning brain.* The cerebral cortex allows us to solve problems, use language and numbers, develop memory, and exercise creativity (Carter, 2009; Howard, 2006). What is important to remember is that problem solving and creativity are associated with this portion of the brain.

When Jane felt threatened with loss of mobility (and freedom!), a toggle called the reticular activating system (RAS), switched her creative, calm learning brain into the "fight, or flight, or freeze" reaction (Howard, 2006, p. 47). Once activated, the hypothalamus pumped out a stress signal in the form of a corticotropin-releasing hormone that began the chemical avalanche triggering fight, flight, or freeze (Stix, 2011).

The switching from the creative learning brain—where one is able to effortlessly flow with ideas or arrive at solutions to problems—to the limbic system wreaks absolute havoc on the state of effortlessness. Remember, when stressed, it's very difficult to experience any sort of ease!! Furthermore, when an individual feels out of control, powerless, or highly controlled, problem solving becomes an automatic brain response "… based on habits, instincts, or other already learned routinized behaviors" (Howard, 2006, p. 512). Our flow within the process of creativity comes to a grinding halt because we are too busy trying to survive rather than attempting to solve the problem at hand! In contrast, when the mind and body are relaxed, the toggle "switches the cortex back on and allows creativity and logic to return to center stage" (Howard, 2006, p. 47).

Immediately after her car broke down, Jane felt fearful as her reptilian brain caused an automatic reaction of panic. Within seconds, numerous functions of the brain interplayed, sending forth stress signals and chemicals while the RAS toggled her thinking from the calm problem solving of the cerebral cortex into the fight, flight, or freeze syndrome of the limbic system. Jane's breathing became shallow and rapid as her limbs tensed up. No longer able to think clearly, Jane began operating on autopilot, defaulting to instinct and habit while allowing someone else to make the decision (i.e., the tow guy). During those stressful moments, Jane was unable to simply realize that she needed more information about auto repair shops. What might have happened had her brain stayed calm?

One solution would have been to leave her car in the parking lot, research other repair garages in the area (after getting a good night's rest), and have the car towed the next day. However, because Jane was operating on autopilot, she was unable to act effortlessly. We might ask ourselves a related question: as a result of ongoing stress, how many of us operate on

"… her reptilian brain caused an automatic reaction of panic. Within seconds, numerous functions of the brain interplayed, sending forth stress signals and chemicals while the RAS toggled her thinking from the calm problem solving of the cerebral cortex into the fight, flight, or freeze syndrome of the limbic system."

automatic pilot—making decisions based on previously acquired habits, instincts, and other learned behaviors?

Finally, these stress land mines have a physical consequence as well. "An emotionalized brain becomes [physically] larger" (Bekhtereva, 1988). This larger brain not only blocks the capacity to perform regular tasks but also hinders our ability to remain within the calm, creative, cerebral cortex. "Usually minor events, such as a delay in the arrival of an airplane or an argument with a co-worker, become major attacks" (Bekhtereva, 1988). If an individual remains stressed, a set of stress hormones (such as cortisol) can actually damage brain cells in the hippocampus and amygdala—both parts of the brain connected to beliefs, emotions, and memories (Stix, 2011). Simply put, it would be wise to catch stress in the act before any real damage is done.

Had Jane remained in the cerebral cortex she could have considered three important questions: With her car in need of repair, what was she about to lose? The obvious answer? Her car. The second and deeper question: What did a functional car actually represent? After careful thought, Jane might have admitted that her car meant autonomy, independence, and freedom to move as she pleased! One final question: would she really lose her freedom of mobility? In a state of calm, Jane might have ultimately answered no. Yes, she might have had to ask friends for a ride or temporarily rely on public transport … but she would have recognized that her independence was not threatened by the fact that she was without a car.

"Once stress is exposed and dismantled, it no longer holds power."

Now you understand how different functions of the brain interplay to create stress and interfere with problem solving. Once stress is exposed and dismantled, it no longer holds power. By making the decision to release struggle and stay calm, you remain in the creative learning brain and pave the way for accessing your state of effortlessness.

JANE TELLS ME I NEED A NEW CHAPTER

Several weeks after Jane's car incident, she called again and said, "You'll need a new chapter." Confused, I asked her to explain. She responded, laughing, "My car won't start again. You'll need a new chapter for your book. However," she continued, "as far as my car is concerned, I don't really care." Of course, I probed further, questioning her statements.

In a nutshell, Jane no longer felt threatened as she did when her car initially broke down. WOW! Jane's reaction—or rather, lack of reaction—marked a huge difference and shift in her perception. With the second breakdown, she was able to quickly acknowledge that her lizard and leopard brains were trying to kick in. She also recognized that fear and anxiety about losing freedom of mobility were vying for her attention. By remaining calm, Jane was able to rationally persuade herself that an automobile breaking down was just that. It did not mean anyone was trying to take away her freedom. These realizations demonstrated that Jane was now problem solving effectively from the cerebral cortex. In dealing with her auto repair Jane stayed calm, cool, and collected as effortless effort, rather than anxiety, was at her fingertips. Very, very nice. Go Jane, go!!

"... she was able to quickly acknowledge that her lizard and leopard brains were trying to kick in. She also recognized that fear and anxiety about losing freedom of mobility were vying for her attention."

4

HECK.

it was just one paper!

The study of creativity is, quite unfortunately, still dominated by a number of rather dated ideas that are either so simplistic that nothing good can possibly come out of them or, given what we know about the brain, factually mistaken.

CHAPTER FOUR

THE RESEARCH PAPER

In the summer of 2009, I decided to write a research paper about how different aspects of the brain affect one's creative state of mind. The concept sounded simple enough for my first graduate-level course. Heck, I had a whole summer to produce just one paper. At the same time, my viewpoint and thoughts about effortlessness were beginning to surface. I began to wonder: "What role does the brain play in the process of creativity? How does the brain inform or influence that state of effortlessness that transcends the traditional creative act?"

I envisioned weaving these related concepts together into an exceptional paper forging an exciting and innovative frontier. A slam dunk seemed inevitable! But then came the questions: What specifically do I research? Creativity? The brain? Stress? Effortlessness? Insight? Neuroplasticity? The more I researched, the further I fell down one rabbit hole after the other. Nevertheless, I was in my bliss, thoroughly enjoying all the new and interesting tidbits of information. At least for the moment, I was a happy camper.

The intent of the paper was to demonstrate that creativity was a subset—as well as the result—of being in a state of effortlessness. At the same time, I wanted to understand and explain the accompanying functions of the brain. But there was one little problem. In terms of neuroscience and creativity, rabbit hole after rabbit hole kept popping up! Finally, in an article titled "Creativity meets neuroscience," the actual issue came to light:

"The intent of the paper was to demonstrate that creativity was a subset—as well as the result—of being in a state of effortlessness."

Creativity is definitely a complex field of research. On the one hand, it pervades almost all areas of our everyday life: It is import in the pedagogical, cultural, and in the scientific domain. Likewise, creativity is advantageous in economy and in the job. On the other hand, no conclusive definition of this mental ability construct has been achieved yet. (Fink, Benedek, Grabner, Staudt, & Neubauer, 2007, p. 1)

After weeks of digging, another researcher shed further (disturbing) light upon my now not-so-simple paper. In 2006 Arne Dietrich wrote an article titled "Who's afraid of a cognitive neuroscience of creativity?" in which he made the following observation:

> *Apart from the enormous amount of fluff out there, the study of creativity is, quite unfortunately, still dominated by a number of rather dated ideas that are either so simplistic that nothing good can possibly come out of them or, given what we know about the brain, factually mistaken.* (Dietrich, 2007, p. 1)

Yikes! While Dietrich acknowledged the value of earlier research on creativity (e.g., the concept of divergence/convergence developed by Guilford in the 1950's), he suggested that, for the most part, forward-thinking research had ground to a halt. As a result, research targeting the phenomenon of creativity had remained undeveloped, especially in areas such as cognitive

"... the study of creativity is, quite unfortunately, still dominated by a number of rather dated ideas that are either so simplistic that nothing good can possibly come out of them or, given what we know about the brain, factually mistaken."

psychology and neuroscience. On a final note, Dietrich suggested that we "do not have the methods or tools to properly bring us to the feet of creativity" (Dietrich, 2007, p. 2). Oh my, my, my. But what about my paper, guys?

With the end of the summer semester quickly approaching, my nerves took a nosedive. Piles of research lay stacked on my desk. How to weave all that research into a coherent paper? Ultimately, stress took over. Effortlessness gave way to my humanness, as the lizard and leopard brains cast me onto an island of survival to fend for myself. Unconsciously and automatically, I returned to old familiar habits.

In the first chapter of this book I mentioned struggling through life by using superhuman amounts of effort. No sleep? No problem. Exercise? Not enough time. Friends and family? Maybe later. Struggle was my old, reliable habit and I was going to push through this deadline regardless of the consequences. I had to "do it all" while maintaining perfectionist standards—not a pretty picture for one attempting to experiment with, and live within the realm of, effortlessness. My process of creativity was long gone, vacationing on a little-known tropical island. And I was not invited.

"My process of creativity was long gone, vacationing on a little known tropical island … I was not invited."

WHO YOU CALLIN' APA?

That summer culminated in enough research material to see me through several additional courses! Looking back, I have to chuckle at the mountain of research that resulted. However, at the time, my deadline loomed like a big, black thundercloud. It was only through sheer will and an enormous amount of effort that I met that deadline.

But then, something not so very funny happened. Although I was quite proud of my paper, it landed on the professor's desk with the grace of a belly flop. The very strict APA style of writing mandated by the graduate school did not quite match my loose and creative interpretations of quoting, citing, and referencing. While naiveté may be bliss, it proved not so in this case. I assumed that those hours of endless research, as reflected in my incredibly lengthy paper, would ultimately triumph. Surely, in terms of APA criteria, the professor would look the other way!

"Oh. My. Goodness. All I could do was crawl back into one of those rabbit holes."

In fact, when my professor called, I was convinced she would congratulate me for the paper's brilliance and explain how to get it published. Imagine my surprise, as well as the extent of my "being taught" within that moment, when she graciously stated, "I am giving you an incomplete. Please redo the paper with the correct APA style. And, oh, by the way ... I did not understand the concept of your paper." Oh. My. Goodness. All I could do was crawl back into one of those rabbit holes.

In hindsight, I admit the paper was indeed a mess. That fall semester found me poring over more library databases, books, and articles—ultimately leading to a greater understanding of the brain, creativity, effortlessness, and stress. Yet, inevitably, ramping up side by side with my writing and research was now the additional stress of completing my incomplete! Heck ... it was still just one paper!! To my way of thinking, however, the work was just the first step leading inexorably to an ingenious trilogy of books. Fortunately, I did learn one other thing. I learned that it would be wise to calm down or my writing would remain a disjointed mess.

Because meditation had once been my go-to place for relaxation, I thought that by resuming a meditation practice, life would become easier. Unfortunately, because I had spent the summer in a constant state of anxiety, none of my usual calming techniques—including meditation—seemed to work. In addition, exercise was still out the window. Sugar had crept its way back into my diet. My eight-to-five job continued to present daily challenges. In short, stress was in the back row throwing rotten tomatoes onto the stage of my brain. I quickly needed to find a new means to quiet my noisy thoughts or I could kiss graduate school good-bye.

WHAT WAS GOING ON IN THE BRAIN?

My challenge as a learner was no different than Jane's stressed response to her broken-down car. As a learner, I felt threatened by the impending deadline, similar to Jane's worry about her means of transportation. While the scenarios were distinctly different, our brains produced the same reactive stress chemicals. The only difference was this: her stress lasted a day or two while mine proved to be ongoing and rampant, adversely affecting me for months.

Stress that is handled within a day or two is one thing. But when stress is chronic, it becomes a subtle yet draining big ol' monkey on one's back. For instance, imagine that your child is experiencing anxiety about passing an English test. This stressful

"As a learner, I felt threatened by the impending deadline, similar to Jane's worry about her means of transportation ... our brains produced the same reactive stress chemicals."

situation, more than likely, will be relieved if a passing grade has been posted. Just like Jane's solution for fixing her car, the problem at hand can be easily solved over a short period of time. However, chronic stress—such as listening to incessant internal dialogue fretting about your retirement or worrying about the economy—has quite a different effect. This type of nagging mind-speak, this kind of unsolvable problem quietly operating in the background and constantly tainting your point of view, is lethal. Too much stress equates to too much struggle. The outcome? No chance for effortlessness. My brain seemed fat, fuzzy, and overwhelmed; I was unable to think clearly. However, I still had to finish that paper!

Unfortunately, at the time of writing the research paper, I did not have the necessary tools for dismantling chronic stress. As a result, my brain obediently protected my body, as the blood moved "away from the cortical areas which are essential to complex thought" (Conyers & Wilson, 2010, p. 33). Instead, all of that blood pumped into my brain's survival areas (Conyers & Wilson, 2010). Consequently, it became incredibly difficult for my thinking brain to process sensory information (Wilson & Conyers, 2010). Yes, I can unequivocally attest to the above statements.

"... nagging mind-speak, this kind of unsolvable problem quietly operating in the background and constantly tainting your point of view, is lethal."

5

THE
dance of the brainwaves

Ever see a skilled jump roper skipping effortlessly while multiple

ropes swing at different times? This image is analogous to

brainwaves working together in synchrony.

CHAPTER FIVE

A SECOND CHANCE

Given a second chance to write my paper, eventually I gingerly crawled out of the rabbit hole. Although quite humbled, I was not defeated. I made a decision to come out of that hole. My new vow became a daily mantra: this paper will not be the end of my grad career—rather, just the beginning! Slowly, my enthusiasm returned.

If a calm mind equated to a highly creative brain, then I would find ways to do just that—become calm! My research had shown that sitting calmly for an hour would also readily assist the writing process. That was great news because even though the calm of meditation had alluded me during the previous semester, I was ready to give the practice another try. Generally, the deliciously soothing salve of meditation had remained with me well through the day. For the moment, it seemed that a cautiously optimistic slam dunk was in progress. Now, in hindsight, I can see that one little problem remained. Where was my Thuse?

Several months passed and I still couldn't get it together to quiet my noisy, nagging, super-chatty brain. My flow was nowhere to be found. My creativity was at an all-time low. I needed to calm down. My research had shown that meditation calmed the brain. And for years I had spent numerous hours in meditative sessions slipping into pure relaxed joy. Yet, recently, I was not meditating. Why? Further, why could I not now sit still for more than a few minutes at a time? In addition, stress continued to nip at my heels. As it turns out, being able to write calmly or to meditate depends not only upon operating from the cerebral cortex (one's creative, learning brain) but also on the

"Several months passed and I still couldn't get it together to quiet my noisy, nagging, super-chatty brain. My flow was nowhere to be found."

amount of electrical current coursing through the brain's lobes. Say what??

THE BRAINWAVE STATES

Inside our electrochemical brain are five unique brainwaves of electrical activity: beta, alpha, theta, delta, and gamma. In fact, this activity can be measured by amplitude and frequency with an electroencephalogram (EEG), a graphic record of brainwaves (Carter, 2009). Within each brainwave frequency we experience a different state of consciousness. For instance, in the beta brainwave state we remain alert and conscious. As we become calmer, the brainwaves slow down, until we enter the next state, a "dreamy" one governed by alpha brainwaves. Even slower are the theta brainwaves, signaling that we are entering the realm of the subconscious. Finally, there are the delta and gamma brainwaves, generally experienced in the unconscious state of deep sleep, although sometimes those brainwaves may be experienced during the waking state. These different brainwaves, although varying in speed, signify sets of neurons that fire somewhat in harmony (Reiner, 2009). One aspect of effortlessness is the ability to allow a harmonious flow of information among all the brainwave states—during any given activity—from the conscious, to the subconscious, and unconscious. It can be done. Therefore, it is quite useful to recognize the importance of all brainwave states.

"These different brainwaves, although varying in speed, signify sets of neurons that fire somewhat in harmony."

THE BETA BRAINWAVE STATE

In the beta brainwave state, "we produce the highest frequency of waves while we are fully conscious" (Dispenza, 2007, p. 463). In the beta, we are wide awake (approximately 13-30 Hz) (Beta wave, 2008). I suspect that in the midst of my initial research, my beta brainwaves were primarily operating at the low range (12.5-16 Hz or cycles per second) and mid-range of the spectrum (16.5-20 Hz) (Beta wave, 2008). Thus, I was a happy camper performing such tasks as browsing through articles or taking notes during class. Easy enough. Bring on the beta? Not quite.

Although operating in the lower frequencies of beta allows us to readily function in the world, the higher beta speeds can be detrimental. Anna Wise, author of *Awakening the Mind: A Guide to Harnessing Your Brainwaves*, states, "While beta is a very important component of our state of consciousness, some people tend to live in those faster frequencies alone, without the support of the lower frequencies" (Wise, 2002, p. 10). As a result of these higher frequencies, we experience an increase in muscle tension as stressful anxiety amplifies. For instance, as I became more anxious about my paper, my beta Hz frequency increased. Ongoing stress hampered my ability to access slower and calmer brainwaves; unfortunately, the effects were just beginning to take their toll.

"Although operating in the lower frequencies of beta allows us to readily function in the world, the higher beta speeds can be detrimental."

CONSUMING TOO MUCH ENERGY

In a five-year research project, Dr. Les Fehmi discovered that when beta brainwaves get amped up, two things happen: 1) we can't think straight and 2) the body starts to consume energy "at a very high and inefficient rate, arousing heart and respiratory rates beyond what is necessary for general daily activities" (Thompson, 2011). Remaining under the influence of high-frequency beta brainwaves for weeks on end is comparable to the experience of a threatened animal constantly on alert for predators. This inefficient use of one's energy and attention weakens the central nervous system, reducing one's capacity to respond to daily challenges from a state of deep resourcefulness (Thompson, 2011).

"Who wants to live in an ongoing high-frequency beta state? As a society, perhaps we need to think twice before allowing stress to rule our lives."

But the major player damaging the brain is cortisol, the "master stress hormone" (Robbins, 2008). Research has also shown "that sustained exposure to cortisol can cause serious damage to the hippocampus, which affects memory, mood regulation, and interpretation to space" (Robbins, 2008, p. 59). Plenty more can be written about the ill affects of stress … but you get the picture.

Now, tell me. Who wants to live in an ongoing high-frequency beta state? As a society, perhaps we need to think twice before allowing stress to rule our lives. If we can recognize when we are in a high beta brainwave state, then we can train ourselves to calm down—or at least to function from a slower beta state. For those choosing to operate from an even calmer state, the next brainwave, alpha, is a wonderful ally.

THE ALPHA BRAINWAVE STATE

Alpha brainwaves vibrate at a lower frequency (approximately 8-12.9 Hz) than beta—which is significant. In the alpha state we are relaxed as we begin to let go of mental control (Alpha wave, 2008). Consider the following statements: "On a molecular plane, creativity can be described as a function of alpha waves, which occur somewhere between alertness and sleep" (Goleman, Kaufman, & Ray, 1992, p. 48). Further, "On the continuum from tight mental self-control to the loss of control we experience in sleep, creativity occurs toward the sleep end of the continuum" (Howard, 2007, p. 616).

There's more. EEG studies have shown that this particular state of creativity is actually focused thinking, albeit dreamy (Claxton, Edwards, & Scale-Constantinou, 2006). Therefore, the phenomenon of creativity is inherent in the alpha brainwave. My alpha state generally happens in the morning, right after I tumble out of bed. My brain has learned to remain in this state between alertness and sleep for two or three hours. I don't talk nor do I think too much. If I am the least bit foggy, I automatically oxygenate my system with deep, long breaths while eating breakfast. Within minutes—and, of course, after my morning coffee—I use the process of creativity to effortlessly flow with my chosen endeavor—my vehicle of writing.

A few hours later, as thoughts about tasks for the day intrude, the beta brainwaves naturally take over. Only then do I pick up the phone to call friends, run errands, or exercise (of course, there are a zillion other types of tasks). Thus during the morning, I have happily and effortlessly fulfilled my creative endeavor for the day. But it takes practice. I have trained my brain to remain in the alpha brainwave state to take full advantage of the inherent creativity within this state.

"My alpha state generally happens in the morning, right after I tumble out of bed. My brain has learned to remain in this state between alertness and sleep for two or three hours."

Now, I have made a choice to live alone and thus can more readily remain within a contemplative space. Nevertheless, even if you have rambunctious children at home making demands on your time and energy, you can still try to carve out a few minutes to focus on entering the alpha brainwave state. Remember: the more time you spend easing into a lower beta frequency and then finally into an alpha brainwave state, the calmer you will be when you focus on your chosen vehicle and practice your process of creativity.

"Theta brainwaves (4-8 Hz) are most conducive to problem solving when synchronized with the alpha brainwaves. High levels of imagery become available. In fact, many in the traditionally creative arts have long utilized the alpha/ theta combo."

THE THETA BRAINWAVE STATE

As helpful as the alpha brainwave state may appear, the theta state is equally beneficial. Theta brainwaves (approximately 4-8 Hz) are most conducive to problem solving when synchronized with the alpha brainwaves. High levels of imagery become available. In fact, many in the traditionally creative arts have long utilized the alpha/theta combo. But first things first. Let me introduce you to theta—gateway to the subconscious. The theta brainwaves are responsible for:

> *dreaming sleep, increased production of catecholamine (vital for learning and memory), increased creativity, integrative, emotional experiences, potential change in behavior, increased retention of learned material, hypnologic imagery, trance, deep meditation, and access to unconscious mind. (Theta wave, 2008)*

The experience of insight illuminating a great idea—one that seems to come out of the blue—results from bursts of theta waves (Dispenza, 2007). When the theta brainwaves begin to synchronize with the alpha, the power of imagination and problem solving prevails. Stress goes on vacation, allowing us to work through complex problems while deriving new concepts from the subconscious mind.

ACCESSING THE ALPHA AND THETA BRAINWAVES

While I was piloting this book and series, one of the workshop participants shared a story that illustrates his understanding of the theta brainwave. As the owner of a popular local dance studio, George was a busy guy. He spent his day in meetings, marketing his business, and attending to financial affairs. In addition, he frequently traveled to ballroom dance competitions.

A couple of weeks before an important competition, George wanted to create an original tango routine for one of his students. However, George was crazy busy, his brain on overload doing the "too much high-beta brain dance." Choreographing an inspired and original dance piece simply wasn't happening. In his words, the routine was just the same ol' same ol'. George's high expectations, combined with the stress of a hectic lifestyle, kept him from accessing his slower and more creative alpha and theta brainwave states. The more George stressed, the less he was able to calm down and focus on solving the problem at hand.

One morning around 4:00 a.m., however, George leapt out of bed, suddenly "seeing" 17 counts of a highly original

"… George was crazy busy, his brain on overload doing the 'too much high-beta brain dance.' Choreographing an inspired and original dance piece simply wasn't happening."

tango. In fact, his inspiration was such that he was easily able to recall the sequence the following day. He happily reported that the routine worked out beautifully. What had happened? This lovely piece of artistry was the result of his brainwaves working in synchrony. The alpha acted as a bridge, helping George recall his creative insight generated by the subconscious theta state. If George had been more practiced, he could have actually accessed his alpha/theta combo while awake. In fact, inventors, artists, and writers have been consciously accessing the alpha/theta brainwave combination for centuries!

"Within the realm of light dozing, countless ideas effortlessly come to the surface as the brain slips into the theta brainwave."

Many literary and visual artists, such as the author Robert Louis Stevenson and the painter Paul Klee, consciously made use of the alpha/theta brainwave state—*hypnagogic* was coined for this state—in which they explored ideas and gained inspiration (Stafford & Webb, 2004). Edgar Allan Poe, another literary giant, wrote of the "fancies" he experienced. "Only when I am on the brink of sleep, with the consciousness that I am so" (Mavromatis, 1987). In fact, Thomas Edison, one of history's most prolific inventors, would sit in a comfortable chair, arms draped over the sides, holding heavy metal balls in his hands. His hands would be poised directly over two metal pans. Edison would purposefully attempt to doze until startled into waking by the sound of balls landing in the pans (Hale-Evans, 2006).

Within the realm of light dozing, countless ideas effortlessly come to the surface as the brain slips into the theta brainwave state. Even the surrealist painter Salvador Dali would try to reach the hypnagogic state as he lay on a sofa, holding a spoon so that it balanced lightly over the edge of a glass. When the spoon clanked, he aroused himself and recorded his ideas (Hale-Evans, 2006).

Working with the hypnagogic state has surprised me again and again with new insights, concepts, and ideas. During the morning when lying in bed half awake, half asleep, I sometimes prolong my waking consciousness to solve problems and explore new perceptions. Although I do not use spoons or metal balls, I've learned to sit and focus on quieting the brain as images roll by. If an idea captures my attention, I make a quick notation before the thought disappears.

As my day progresses, if a need for rest arises, I quiet my thoughts through light meditation. Wonderful ideas spring forth as the beta state relinquishes its hold, allowing the alpha and theta to relax my fatigued brain. Ten to thirty minutes later my body is completely refreshed. While the ability to become consciously aware of the theta state is quite powerful, the next brainwave state produces the deep rest that the body needs.

THE DELTA BRAINWAVE STATE

The delta brainwave state occurs during unconscious dreamless sleep (approximately 0.5-3.9 Hz). This state has also been likened to the bliss of deep meditation. In delta we restore, replenish, and rejuvenate (Delta, 2008). This state can also be available during our waking world. The delta, in concert with the alpha and theta, allows us to be more aware of unconscious information that is not readily available to the conscious mind. Research has shown that individuals gifted with highly intuitive abilities

"In delta we restore, replenish, and rejuvenate. This state can also be available during our waking world. The delta, in concert with the alpha and theta, allows us to be more aware of unconscious information that is not readily available to the conscious mind."

usually display measurable delta brainwaves during their waking moments.

With delta, our intuitive radar scans the environment to provide information that translates into a sense of deep inner knowing. For instance, consider the last time you were able to walk into a room and pick up on unspoken vibes from the group sitting at the conference table. That's delta. Remember George, the owner of the dance studio discussed earlier within this chapter? He has an uncanny ability to assist dance partners, not only by teaching them a salsa or waltz but also by being a kind of a therapist—knowing just the right thing to say at the right time. His clientele marvel at how he just senses their troubles. More than likely, George is so focused and calm while teaching that his alpha and theta combine with his intuitive delta brainwaves. This keen combination allows him to quietly intuit his clients' mental and emotional essence.

"... consider the last time you were able to walk into a room and pick up on unspoken vibes from the group sitting at the conference table. That's delta."

THE GAMMA BRAINWAVE STATE

Of all the brainwaves, gamma is the most elusive. In fact, gamma brainwaves are often overlooked or excluded from discussions regarding brainwaves. Yet, these brainwaves are exceedingly powerful. Its oscillations are the fastest: approximately 40 Hz to 70 Hz. Most people only experience these waves "in very short bursts during REM sleep and, rarely, in waking cognition" (Reiner, 2009). With such rarity, why would we care about this brainwave?

In June 2002, Antoine Lutz studied a French-born monk, Mattieu Ricard, who had meditated for 10,000 hours during his lifetime (Geirland, 2006). During the study, Lutz positioned 128 electrodes on Ricard's head, then asked him to specifically meditate on "unconditional loving-kindness and compassion" (Geirland, 2006). The results were astounding. Lutz immediately observed the measurements of 40 cycles per second (gamma brainwaves), indicating that Ricard was experiencing intensely focused thought (Geirland, 2006). Lutz's research crew was convinced something was wrong with the equipment or with their methods.

The researchers then brought in additional monks, as well as a control group of students who were completely inexperienced with meditation (Geirland, 2006). The resulting data indicated that the monks (all experienced meditators) indeed produced gamma brainwaves 30 times stronger than that of the students (Geirland, 2006). In addition, "larger areas of the meditators' brains were active—particularly the prefrontal cortex area which is the section responsible for positive emotions" (Geirland, 2006). How do these findings apply to us?

While it is impractical for us to sit and meditate for years in a Himalayan cave, we can still appreciate the value of gamma brainwaves and try to recognize their existence within our lives. For instance, while discussing gamma brainwaves with my friend, Lynn, I noticed she was having difficulty grasping the relevance of gamma in her own life. In Lynn's words, she "related more to the students than the monks." Then she had an aha! moment. Lynn recalled having had a number of intense, compassionate, and powerful dreams resolving a painful experience from years before. Suddenly she blurted out, "My dreams were a burst of

"While it is impractical for us to sit and meditate for years in a Himalayan cave, we can still appreciate the value of gamma brainwaves and try to recognize their existence within our lives."

gamma!" Lynn's realization—that she had had a direct experience with the gamma brainwaves—sparked her interest in cultivating further experiences with the gamma. Who knows? She may even become a monk!

David Dobbs, a science journalist writing for *Scientific American*, reports that the gamma brainwaves produce "not relaxation but an intense though serene attention" (Dobbs, 2005). He further states that gamma synchrony is "increasingly associated with robust brain function and the synthesis of activity that we call the mind" (Dobbs, 2005). Cultivating gamma brainwaves not only serves to strengthen our focus but also enhances optimism and compassion. We now know that we do not have to be meditating monks to attain the state of gamma. However, we do need to access and utilize all brainwaves simultaneously to experience harmonious brainwave synchrony. Then the question becomes: why is brainwave synchrony so important?

"Cultivating gamma brainwaves not only serves to strengthen our focus but also enhances optimism and compassion."

SYNCHRONY OF THE BRAINWAVES

Ever see a skilled jump roper skipping effortlessly while multiple ropes swing at different times? This is analogous to brainwaves working together in synchrony. Anna Wise's research demonstrates that the prerequisite for a high-performance mind "is to be able to have an open flow of information between the conscious, subconscious, and unconscious mind" (Wise, 2002, p. 8). Wise also notes that "the brain-wave patterns of high performance, of creativity and the bursts of peak experience" are the same patterns as those experienced by Himalayan monks practicing meditation for years (Wise, 2002, p. 4). She further states that combining these brainwave patterns in the "right combination and proportion" creates the blocks to build our consciousness (Wise, 2002). Okay, so what do synchronized brainwaves have to do with effortlessness? And, with the state of Thuse? Glad you asked.

At the beginning of this chapter, I mentioned that an aspect of effortlessness is the ability to allow information to flow from the conscious to the subconscious to the unconscious. I also remarked that this flow of information is possible during *any* activity. In short, can be simultaneously and easily accessed and, when this happens, we find ourselves in the *process* of creativity. This synchrony is one aspect that helps lead us into the state of effortlessness. Now, I know … this sounds like a tall order. And, one might assume that this state of synchrony is reserved only for Zen masters and high-performance people. But, actually, that's not correct.

The ability to synchronize the brainwaves is available to anyone making a concerted effort to understand and utilize his/her process of creativity. It is imperative to slow down that fast beta brainwave—so we may then more easily access the alpha/theta and then harmonize with some level of the delta/gamma. But how does a stressed mother taking care of rowdy children or an employee jumping through multiple hoops to fill an overseas order slow down high frequency beta brainwaves during a stressful day?

One solution: to engage in a daily activity meant to slow down the high frequency beta brainwaves, whether it takes five

"… engage in a daily activity meant to slow down the high frequency beta brainwaves, whether it takes five minutes or several hours."

minutes or several hours. The list of such activities is endless: sitting in silence while watching the breath rise and fall, listening to relaxing music or, even better, listening to music written specifically to synchronize the brainwaves. Other more physical activities might include yoga, tai chi, or chi gong. Any activity that focuses and calms your brain while also allowing you to feel refreshed and invigorated is your tool. Discover your own method of calming overstimulated beta brainwaves and practice it on a regular basis. For super-busy people, just start with five minutes.

"As a result of lowered stress, your brainwaves are more closely synchronized and, therefore, you more easily slip into the process of creativity."

What are the detriments of not training the brainwaves to operate at a slower frequency throughout the day? Well ... we're stressed. So we come home from an 8-to-5 job, zone out by drinking a couple glasses of wine, or end up watching a little too much TV. We do anything but what we truly want to do.

Now, what are benefits of training the beta brainwaves to slow down? Your stressful tasks during the day become more effortless. Then, because you are less stressed, you have more energy to do what you truly want to do. As a result of lowered stress, your brainwaves are more closely synchronized and, therefore, you more easily slip into the process of creativity.

While we cannot know for certain if our brainwaves are indeed synchronized, we do know when we are effortlessly flowing with an activity or when we're having a stressed-out, difficult time. Whether taking care of family responsibilities and a house full of kids, studying for a difficult exam, or trying to meet an impossible deadline, challenging activities will always be part of our daily lives. Training the brain to be calm and focused allows us to be that much closer to the process of creativity and ultimately to the state of Thuse.

We all live busy lives. Yet, it is imperative that we become acutely aware whenever we begin to operate from a high beta brainwave state. With this awareness comes a chance to pause, breathe deeply for a few minutes, and then perhaps make the choice to participate more calmly. In summary, letting go of stress by becoming calmer and more focused allows for brainwave synchrony, which facilitates the process of creativity that leads to the state of effortlessness and ultimately to experiencing the Mind of Thuse.

6

THE
rosebush & the thistle

When we consciously develop new habits, we create parallel synaptic paths, and even entirely new brain cells, that can jump our trains of thought onto new, innovative tracks.

Chapter Six

COLIN PERFORMS AN EXPERIMENT

As a young girl, I was enchanted by Frances Hodgson Burnett's book entitled *The Secret Garden*. In fact, I feigned illness for three days in order to stay in bed and read it from cover to cover. At the time, my eleven-year-old brain had no clue of the seeds being planted. Forty-something years later, the book crossed my hands once again. This time, as I curled up with my iPad late into the night, moments of joy accompanied a new understanding of its simple yet profound message. The story, set in England around the turn of the 20th century, goes something like this: two spoiled, insensitive children, Mary and Colin, are transformed by events occurring within a secret garden. During the novel, young Colin—previously friendless and unable to walk—decides to perform an experiment. Every day, whilst carousing in the garden with his new friends, he attempts to move up and out of his wheelchair, to stand without assistance. Every day his body responds with just a tad more movement. At the end of the novel, Colin's father returns from a lengthy trip to discover that his son can now not only stand but walk, as well.

Although *The Secret Garden* is considered a children's novel, the book offers a compelling message for the individual moving towards effortlessness—a message related to the power of thought. Let's read some excerpts from chapter 27:

> In each century since the beginning of the world
> wonderful things have been discovered. In the last
> century more amazing things were found out than in
> any century before. In this new century hundreds of

"At first people refuse to believe that a strange new thing can be done, then they begin to hope it can be done, then they see it can be done—then it is done and all the world wonders why it was not done centuries ago."

"One of the new things people began to find out in the last century was that thoughts— just mere thoughts—are as powerful as electric batteries—as good for one as sunlight is, or as bad for one as poison."

things still more astounding will be brought to light. At first people refuse to believe that a strange new thing can be done, then they begin to hope it can be done, then they see it can be done—then it is done and all the world wonders why it was not done centuries ago. One of the new things people began to find out in the last century was that thoughts—just mere thoughts— are as powerful as electric batteries—as good for one as sunlight is, or as bad for one as poison. To let a sad thought or a bad one get into your mind is as dangerous as letting a scarlet fever germ get into your body. If you let it stay there after it has got in you may never get over it as long as you live.

So long as Mistress Mary's mind was full of disagreeable thoughts about her dislikes and sour opinions of people and her determination not to be pleased by or interested in anything, she was a yellow-faced, sickly, bored and wretched child. Circumstances, however, were very kind to her, though she was not at all aware of it. They began to push her about for her own good. When her mind gradually filled itself with robins, and moorland cottages crowded with children, with queer crabbed old gardeners and common little Yorkshire housemaids, with springtime and with secret gardens coming alive day by day, and also with a moor boy and his "creatures," there was no room left for the disagreeable thoughts which affected her liver and her digestion and made her yellow and tired.

*So long as Colin shut himself up in his room
and thought only of his fears and weakness and his
detestation of people who looked at him and reflected
hourly on humps and early death, he was a hysterical
half-crazy little hypochondriac who knew nothing of
the sunshine and the spring and also did not know
that he could get well and could stand upon his feet if
he tried to do it. When new beautiful thoughts began
to push out the old hideous ones, life began to come
back to him, his blood ran healthily through his veins
and strength poured into him like a flood. His scientific
experiment was quite practical and simple and there
was nothing weird about it at all. Much more surprising
things can happen to any one who, when a disagreeable
or discouraged thought comes into his mind, just has
the sense to remember in time and push it out by
putting in an agreeable determinedly courageous one.
Two things cannot be in one place. (Burnett, 1911)*

"... Mary's physical appearance—yellow-faced and sickly—was actually a physical manifestation of her constant naysaying thoughts."

Burnett emphasizes the danger of a negative thought by comparing it to a germ making a body ill. For instance, Burnett suggested that Mary's physical appearance—yellow-faced and sickly—was actually a physical manifestation of her constant naysaying thoughts. In addition, Burnett attempted to point out that Colin's ill health, and the fact that he was bedridden, also resulted from his repugnant thoughts.

Finally, Burnett ends his lovely excerpt with: "Where you tend a rose, my lad, a thistle cannot grow" (Burnett, 1911).

So what does this statement mean? *Really* mean? From my perspective, Colin's daily new habit—cultivating his desired ability to walk—is symbolized by the healthy rosebush. On the other hand, the thistle symbolizes Colin's pessimistic belief that he will always be confined to a bed and wheelchair. Colin could either perceive himself as an invalid or a young boy able to walk; however, both sets of thoughts could not exist simultaneously. As nature so beautifully illustrates, a thistle cannot grow in the same exact spot as a rosebush, particularly when the rose is tended with care.

"... knowing the concept and applying it to daily life in each and every moment—is a completely different ballgame. It takes practice to stop a negative thought in its tracks— a lot of practice."

Now let's do our own experiment. For starters, try contemplating two opposing thoughts at the same exact time. Ouccch! My brain goes on "tilt" when I try. Similar to gardening, when one is tending the brain with quiet, consistently calm and assured thoughts, those anxious, dark and worrisome thoughts simply have no room to flourish. Chances are you already know and understand this concept. However, knowing the concept and applying it to daily life in each and every moment is a completely different ballgame. It takes practice to stop a negative thought in its tracks—a lot of practice.

Colin's body responded well in response to his changing thought processes. With consistent practice, he went from a bedridden invalid to a healthy boy easily able to walk. Was this magic? A miracle? Is Colin's story a persuasive testimonial, underscoring the importance of cultivating beautiful rosy thoughts rather than negative, thistle-like thoughts? In this manner, both Colin and Mary were able to develop more positive frames of mind when visiting a blossoming spring garden and being supported by new friendships. These new daily activities became their daily habits.

Burnett briefly alludes to the fact that Colin's effort was a scientific experiment. Indeed, this is correct. What Colin experienced is based in pure science. How? Let's explore the effects of habitual thoughts on the brain.

HEY NEURON, WAKE UP!

Neuroplasticity research has proven that—with focused and consistent thought—one can retrain the brain to produce such "miracles" as Colin's ability to walk. Although numerous physiological systems contributed to Colin's recovery, let us look closely at what transpired in Colin's brain. Specifically, how did his brain cultivate change via the transmission of information from billions of brain cells called neurons?

While we are sleeping, eating, walking, talking, having fun, or working, our brains are filled with busy little guys and gals constantly moving information to each other through electrochemical impulses. This information transmission is the function of a neuron. When two neurons come together to communicate a message, they literally "fire off" or synapse with each other via an electrical signal. This firing then releases a chemical messenger known as a neurotransmitter (Howard, 1999). This concept is similar to Burnett's analogy of thoughts being as powerful as electric batteries.

Further, these neurons work together to build a learned habit. This happens when an active neuron stimulates a nearby resting neuron. The active, awake neuron knocks on the door of

"When two neurons come together to communicate a message, they literally 'fire off' or synapse with each other via an electrical signal. … This concept is similar to Burnett's analogy of thoughts being as powerful as electric batteries."

its resting neighbor, "Hey neuron! Wake up! Come out to play." At first the nearby sleepy neuron pokes its head out the door to acknowledge the neighbor by yelling back and firing at random. Yet, after only one or two firings, the neuron yawns and returns to rest. Nevertheless, the random firings of this neuron indicates the beginning of learning something new. But more important, it is the beginning of the process of change that starts with just one single thought—such as Colin's decision to participate in an experiment (trying to walk).

As the active, yelling neuron keeps shouting to its napping neighbor, a habit slowly develops. New thoughts replace old ones. Eventually the sleepy neuron really wakes up, goes outside to play, and fires in unison with the playful and active neuron. Through subsequent firings between these two neurons, chemical changes occur sending out messages to the body. The newly awakened neuron begins to yell at yet another next-door resting neighbor. This process of one neuron waking the other continues until every neuron "kid" on the block is wide awake and firing (Carter, 2009; Howard, 1999).

In turn, the awakened street of neurons yells at the sleeping "kid" on the next block. Street by street, neighborhood by neighborhood, the whole town is awakened and the business of building a new neural network is underway. Neurons that fire together will wire together (Carter, 2009). In his efforts to learn how to walk, Colin was simply, yet consistently, working his neurons!

This waking up, firing, and wiring of multiple neurons entrenches a new behavior, habit, or thought. Through repetition,

"Street by street, neighborhood by neighborhood, the whole town is awakened and the business of building a new neural network is underway. Neurons that fire together will wire together."

a neural pathway or "rut" is formed within our brains. The formation of habits (desired or not) is simply the result of neurons firing together (Carter, 2009). Imagine following the same path while skiing down a ski slope every day, all day. Eventually a rut will be formed in the snow. In the same manner, a new habit or habitual thought creates a neural rut and solidly becomes a part of our physical being.

CHANGE, CHANGE, CHANGE!

Neuroplasticity involves the ability to reorganize neural networks and thereby redirect established pathways of habits and thoughts onto new routes. According to science writer Janet Rae-Dupree, "Brain researchers have discovered that when we consciously develop new habits, we create parallel synaptic paths, and even entirely new brain cells, that can jump our trains of thought onto new, innovative tracks" (Rae-Dupree, 2008). Rae-Dupree suggests, "Rather than dismissing ourselves as unchangeable creatures of habit, we can instead direct our own change by consciously developing new habits" (Rae-Dupree, 2008). In other words, an "old dog," with focus, tenacity, and repetition, can learn new tricks and thereby create a new thought pattern leading to a new habit. Once a new habit is created, we are forever changed. Right? Well, yes and no.

Although our habits may be changed by the formation of a new neural pathway, old pathways related to old habits are not automatically erased from the brain. Ann Graybiel, the Walter A. Rosenblith Professor of Neuroscience in MIT's Department of Brain and Cognitive Sciences, reports this phenomenon in her

"... when we consciously develop new habits, we create parallel synaptic paths, and even entirely new brain cells, that can jump our trains of thought onto new, innovative tracks."

research findings, "We knew that neurons can change their firing patterns when habits are learned, but it is startling to find that these patterns reverse when the habit is lost, only to recur again as soon as something kicks off the habit again" (Delude, 2005). Yikes! Is it any wonder that most New Year's resolutions don't stick?

Neuroplasticity does not have the ability to differentiate between new and old neural pathways, between new habits and old habits, between new thoughts and old thoughts. Because neuroplasticity cannot build a roadblock to the old pathway, it's fairly easy to jump tracks to the previous neural network and, therefore, reactivate an old habit. So ... how do we make the new habit permanent? For starters, we move out of our comfort zones on a regular basis—by taking ongoing, small risks while building the new habit. Sound simple?

RISK TAKING: NOT TOO BIG

What exactly is a risk? A risk is the perception and/or possibility of negative effects such as loss or harm that might result from taking an action. The risk may involve outcomes that range from actual physical danger to mere perceived threats of loss; notwithstanding, the thought of taking risks may make one uncomfortable and, therefore, prone to "thistle" thoughts that trigger fight, flight, or freeze. For many of us, our daily lives include such risks as purchasing a new house in a volatile job market or incurring tens of thousands of dollars in student loans while attending college. Even engaging in a new relationship is

"We knew that neurons can change their firing patterns when habits are learned, but it is startling to find that these patterns reverse when the habit is lost, only to recur again as soon as something kicks off the habit again."

considered a risk. Taking risks means stepping out of our comfort zone. Now, why would we want to do that?

From my perspective, we must learn to take risks in order to confront ongoing disquieting thoughts. What exactly do I mean by that sentence? Many of us walk around with tiny nagging thoughts that often cause unconscious and subconscious discomfort. An example: a nagging thought may stem from a disagreement you had with a friend ten years ago. You miss this friend and would love to talk with her/him but to make that phone call is quite uncomfortable and thus, a risk. Why is it a risk? Because by making that phone call, you expose yourself to the possibility of feeling more pain. Yet, that is only the perceived threat. The reality may be entirely different; in other words, your perceptions might not be true.

"The purpose of taking risks is to build courage. The more risks you take, the more courage you develop … and have at your fingertips."

But what if your perceptions are true? What if the friend hangs up on your phone call? Although this might be hurtful, the outcome is not what matters. What matters is that you took the risk. The purpose of taking risks is to build *courage.* The more risks you take, the more courage you develop … and have at your fingertips. And how does this relate to the process of creativity? Well … the process of creativity requires ongoing courage to do those things you previously thought to be too difficult.

Although there is great benefit in taking risks, some of us can get sideswiped by the size of a risk. I actually prefer taking small risks. Why? Well, large risks can easily toggle the reactive brain. In her book, *This Year I Will* ... M. J. Ryan states, "Whenever we initiate change, even a positive one, we activate fear in our emotional brain" (Ryan, 2006, p. 77). We now know that when an individual is threatened by even the smallest change, "the blood moves away from the cortical areas of the brain, which are essential to complex thought, into the survival areas of the brain" (Conyers & Wilson, 2010, p. 33). Risks that are too big can easily initiate the fight, flight, or freeze syndrome.

The resulting fear can trigger previous "thistle" thoughts in which our old habit—the other neural pathway—takes over. To illustrate my point, think about how many times you (or someone you know) may have attempted to write a business plan around an amazing idea but—much like the resting neuron—eventually abandoned the activity to return and watch a little too much TV. Why? Perhaps the risk was too big. Or, perhaps the risk entailed forgoing a "traditional" approach to solving the problem at hand in favor of a new and novel approach (Bowden & Jung-Beeman, 2006). Changing a learned habit in order to "see" a new solution requires courage because the change registered in the brain signals danger!

"Changing a learned habit in order to 'see' a new solution requires courage because the change registered in the brain signals danger!"

Keep in mind that the brain reacts to risk in proportion to the size of the perceived threat. If the perceived threat appears huge, the thought of taking that risk also seems huge and significantly increased reactions occur within the brain. In fact, the brain may well try to avoid even considering taking that risk. On the other hand, if the brain perceives the risk as small, less reactive activity occurs. The smaller the risk, the more willing the brain is to take those risks. The more risks that are taken, the more courage will be built. In fact, something very curious happens when we are able to step out of our comfort zones on a consistent basis.

When we take small risks, we can stealthily activate our process of creativity. In a *New York Times* article, author Rae-Dupree states, "In fact, the more new things we try—the more we step outside our comfort zone—the more inherently creative we become, both in the workplace and in our personal lives" (Rae-Dupree, 2008). Rae-Dupree's research supports our concept of the process of creativity. That creativity is not just for traditionally creative individuals! That creativity is something we can all experience by trying new things and taking risks. Just remember, taking small risks, and doing so consistently, shifts us out of our comfort zones into the process of creativity.

"... the more we step outside our comfort zone—the more inherently creative we become, both in the workplace and in our personal lives."

7

struggle to effortlessness

Unlike struggle, the stage of effort allows us to enter into the
process of creativity. Why? With effort, the task may be difficult.
There may be a lot of work involved but you are partaking in the
task with a calm, nonreactive brain.

Chapter Seven

SUCKER PUNCHED

Several years ago, when I first began teaching the content of this book to college students, some of them voiced rather strong opinions. While writing the book, I had entertained great expectations—surely everyone would love the results! However, during an initial pilot, on a very public forum, a couple of students harshly critiqued the work from beginning to end. Ugh! I felt sucker punched. Anybody stumbling onto the forum could read these quite critical posts.

As a result, that summer found me anxiously waiting for the semester to end. I wanted those particular students out of my classroom and off the forum. Their strong reactions triggered my unwanted "thistle" thoughts of insecurity that turned into anger and blame. How dare they not love the book!! Feeling threatened, my brain went into the protective fight, flight, or freeze mode. In addition, my beta brainwaves remained in a high frequency state almost all summer. The results? On a primal level, I wanted to head for the hills and hide. Regarding my process of creativity, it came to an abrupt halt. Is this sounding familiar?

In hindsight, those students were right. They had insisted that it takes tremendous effort to attend classes, complete assignments, and (for many students) work to support a family. At that time, my pilot book only focused on the ideal aspects of effortless effort and effortlessness. Well, yes, I now stand corrected. Thank you to my vocal, honest students who taught me invaluable lessons!!

What I began to understand were the following: 1) my students were mistaking struggle for effort (I had not drawn

"On a primal level, I wanted to head for the hills and hide. Regarding my process of creativity, it came to an abrupt halt. Is this sounding familiar?"

a clear distinction between the two) and 2) I had neglected to convey the role of effort within the process of creativity. In short, we do need to address the distinction between *struggle* and *effort* in order to fully grasp the ideal aspect (effort) that is part of the process of creativity. What needs to be emphasized is that, when participating in a new endeavor or project and subsequent problem solving, it's possible to experience up to four distinct stages: 1) struggle, 2) effort, 3) effortless effort, and 4) effortlessness. Although we've touched on these stages in previous chapters, it's time to clarify further.

One particularly important point is this: the way in which we respond to situations during the first two stages (struggle and effort) determines, in large part, whether or not we can access our process of creativity. Remember, it is the process of creativity that leads to effortless effort … and ultimately to effortlessness.

In the case of the students' criticisms, my reactions caused me to almost drown in struggle. I was unaware and unconscious and therefore, unable to "see" my reactions. Their criticism had hit like a bolt of lightning; indeed, I had expected that, at the crucial pilot stage, they would fully embrace the book's philosophy. Heck, I had been effortlessly writing for months. But this jolt brought about a crisis of confidence. When my expectations were not met, insecurity and negative emotions flooded my brain. Reactions from the "thistle" brain tossed my process of creativity overboard. Hence began my struggle!!

Had I recognized the need to be in the stage of effort rather than that of struggle, I would have remembered that the

"In short, we do need to address the distinction between struggle and effort in order to fully grasp the ideal aspect (effort) that is part of the process of creativity."

purpose of piloting a book is to be able to adjust and change—based on criticism. Had I been able to see that I, too, was *learning*, then student criticism would have been much more welcome. In other words, during times of change (when risk taking or beginning a new endeavor), we have the potential to become less reactive if we will only acknowledge the need to be in a stage of effort rather than struggle. This leads to a key question: how do we distinguish between the stage of effort and the stage of struggle?

I have addressed the notion of struggle in previous chapters. Struggle looks like the ongoing stress I experienced when writing my first graduate paper, or Jane's initial reactions when her car broke down, or my urge to run from my students when feeling threatened by their posts. Struggle begins when expectations are not being met. Chances are, if you have a strong preference or belief that is not being met—as my strong desire for all my students to love the book—you are most likely in struggle.

In turn, angst, worry, fear, or any negative emotion will amplify the stage of struggle and thus roadblock your entrance into the process of creativity. In addition, even if you are already in the process of creativity, struggle will cause you to be thrown out of it.

Unlike struggle, effort is a *conscious recognition that we're experiencing or learning something new*. In the stage of effort, we are exploring new territory. You may or may not enjoy the task at hand but engaging in the task is a necessary part of effort. Further, in the stage of effort, we may need to repeat a task 20 times before it becomes easier and easier to perform.

"... effort is a conscious recognition that we're experiencing or learning something new. In the stage of effort, we are exploring new territory."

This repetition builds a neural network that, in turn, becomes an ingrained habit or new learned behavior.

Unlike struggle, the stage of effort allows us to enter into the process of creativity. Why? With effort, the task may be difficult. There may be a lot of work involved but you are partaking in the task with a calm, nonreactive brain. Once you have achieved the new learned behavior, performing the task becomes easier than not—effortless effort begins. So ... what to do when recognizing you are in struggle? Well, you should pat yourself on the back for actually seeing that you are in struggle because the reactive brain will blind you to that. This recognition becomes a pivotal moment of power. You now have a choice to step from struggle to effort.

"Unlike struggle, the stage of effort allows us to enter into the process of creativity. Why? With effort, the task may be difficult. There may be a lot of work involved but you are partaking in the task with a calm, nonreactive brain."

At that point, you can ask yourself: "Do I need help, or more time to contemplate the problem?" or "Do I have enough input or research?" If none of these questions eases the brain's agitation, then self-reflective questions are in order:

- *"Why am I anxious?"*
- *"What am I expecting?"*
- *"What do I perceive will be lost?"*
- *"Can I let go of my expectations?"*
- *"What tool(s) do I have to help me calm down?"*

These simple yet surprisingly powerful questions may help unearth why you are struggling. Answering them is the second step to stepping out of struggle. To further illustrate, let's take a look at an example that differentiates struggle and effort and also begins to show how effortless effort leads into effortlessness.

THE SEESAW OF STRUGGLE AND EFFORT

When I decided to design and produce my website, that particular project then became my vehicle for entering into the process of creativity. Although my skill set included traditional, reliable methods for building a site, I was intrigued by newer content management systems such as Joomla, Drupal, and WordPress (thank you, open source code developers!). In the beginning, while updating to the newer technology, my brain literally hurt from so much focus and effort. My neurons were having a major block party from all that learning!

Initially, I was in the stage of effort, often spending several hours to solve a seemingly simple problem. However, I was happily and eagerly learning new information. Then one evening, my brain went "tilt." One too many problems presented themselves, each requiring a tremendous amount of time. Just thinking about my website for the next few days produced angst and stress. Further, the simple realization that I was smack-dab in a learning curve evaded me. Nagging thoughts persisted: "This website is such a huge pain!" and "I'll never finish this web site!!" and "Maybe this book project and the workshops are better left for another day." No doubt about it. I had succumbed to anxiety and irritation. These emotions, in turn, had triggered old, unwelcome patterns of perfectionism and impatience. Yes, struggle was up front and center! I had to get rid of those "thistle" thoughts and get rid of them quickly—or struggle would remain. But how?

When in struggle, I find that asking self-reflective questions helps to reveal old stuck emotions, perceptions, and

"No doubt about it. I had succumbed to anxiety and irritation. These emotions, in turn, had triggered old, unwelcome patterns of perfectionism and impatience. Yes, struggle was up front and center!"

beliefs. But because the brain is producing an avalanche of stress chemicals, it takes significant effort on my part to quiet the angst. I have to dig into my personal tool kit for techniques to quiet the brain. By implementing these techniques, I can return to working within the stage of effort and enter again the process of creativity.

BUILDING YOUR EFFORTLESS TOOL KIT

Please keep in mind that everyone will have his/her own personal strategies and techniques for working with struggle. However, when quieting struggle, here are five guidelines to follow: 1) recognize/acknowledge that you are actually in struggle, 2) take time to uncover the perceptions and beliefs that form your "thistle" thoughts, 3) use your personal techniques or tools to identify and perhaps express the emotions behind such "thistle" thoughts, 4) build a new neural network based on thoughts or a statement that replaces the "thistle" thoughts; and 5) muster up feelings such as gratitude or joy to accompany the new thoughts and/or statement. The example below illustrates these contemplative guidelines in action.

Here's how it worked for me regarding the frustrating website experience. First, I had to realize that I was in struggle … and then ask: why am I experiencing so much pressure and stress? Impatience had become an overriding emotion even though my deadlines were self-imposed. However, because I had been working on and talking about this book for years, I felt under tremendous pressure!! What was the holdup? In a nutshell: while I had generous support from family, friends, co-workers,

"First, I had to realize that I was in struggle … and then ask: why am I experiencing so much pressure and stress? Impatience had become an overriding emotion even though my deadlines were self-imposed."

and helpers during this process, I was scared of putting my life's work in the public eye—and being exposed!! People would talk!! All these nagging "thistle" thoughts opened the gate to my old neural networks of perfectionism. Once I realized that I would be just fine, even if the book and workshops attracted a fair share of critics, the pressure lifted. Step one complete.

Second, to neutralize the fear of being exposed, I used several rounds of Emotional Freedom Technique tapping (EFT) to release trapped beliefs and emotions.* This effective technique quickly and easily accessed my hidden thoughts, beliefs, and emotions. From this technique came the realization that I expected the site to be perfect. In addition, I was able to consider what would be lost if I didn't finish the site—my perception of professional respect from others. Once these emotions were released, I realized that the site did not have to be perfect and that my personal esteem would remain intact even if I lost professional respect. With these insights, I released fearful emotions. Step two complete.

Third, I realized that I needed to synchronize my brainwaves. While struggling with the site, my brain was unable to access an alpha/theta brainwave state. To lower my high frequency beta brainwaves and nudge myself into an alpha/theta state, I repeatedly listened to a musical track that I created—one specifically designed to synchronize brainwaves in order to enter the process of creativity. (This musical track and others are included in the workbook series). By lowering the frequency of

"To lower my high frequency beta brainwaves and nudge myself into an alpha/theta state, I repeatedly listened to a musical track that I created—one specifically designed to synchronize brainwaves in order to enter the process of creativity."

* *http://www.emofree.com/eft/overview.html*

the brainwaves into an alpha/theta state, I was able to work on the site with a much calmer brain. Step three complete.

Finally, I began to focus my thoughts (in a positive direction) regarding the website by silently repeating a phrase that had special meaning for me. The phrase, combined with purposeful feelings of ease and joy, was meant to interfere with, and halt, the chatter of "thistle" thoughts. While I have used many phrases—from both Eastern and Western philosophies and teachings—in the case of my website, I used a phrase shared by Rennie Davis, a lecturer on self-awareness: "Everything is better than you can even imagine."

Throughout the day, I silently repeated that phrase while mustering ease and joy whenever mentally envisioning my website. In addition, I made sure my breathing was deep and relaxed when contemplating the next set of website problems to be solved. With my thoughts now properly focused, I had completed the requisite steps to recognize and remove struggle—at which point I entered once again into the process of creativity. The results? Within a couple of days I began to solve problems more quickly. Furthermore, I started to enjoy working on the site again because I had shifted away from struggle and once again into the stage of effort.

After I had put in the effort to learn the nuances of Joomla, then I began to experience ease with the task at hand. With this ease my efforts became more effortless than not. Combined with a more balanced mental and emotional body, I was able to operate from a low frequency beta or alpha brainwave state. I had entered into the stage of effortless effort.

"Within a couple of days I began to solve problems more quickly. Furthermore, I started to enjoy working on the site again because I had shifted away from struggle and once again into the stage of effort."

Effortless effort is the stage in which we have moved beyond effort and are (more effortlessly than not) involved with the task at hand. We've learned how to do the task and, for the most part, feel confident that we know what we are doing. This stage walks hand in hand with effort as we toggle between the two until we're able to fully remain in effortless effort. Although this stage is integral to the process of creativity, we only remain in effortless effort a short time because it is a fulcrum point within the process of creativity. Once we leave behind effort and begin experiencing ease, we quickly enter into effortlessness.

While building the website, I studied online videos in order to understand how to solve a particular coding problem (effort). While acquiring this skill, my brain was hard at work building a new neural network (effort). With the newly ingrained information, continuing the task at hand—while also solving similar, related problems—became more effortless than not (effortless effort). Now … here is the interesting point about effortless effort.

The seesaw stage—between effort and effortless effort—may last for a few minutes or for a much longer time before one is more effortlessly than not involved with solving the problem at hand. As a point of emphasis: the seesaw effect between effort and effortless effort may last for hours, days, or even months before effortlessness takes hold. However, when you do move once and for all from effort into effortless effort—and remain there—effortlessness is quick to follow.

Effortless effort is the gateway to delightful effortlessness that include timelessness and endless energy. Regarding the

"The intuitive mind is a sacred gift and the rational mind is a faithful servant. We have created a society that honors the servant and has forgotten the gift." —Einstein

concept of flow (which I consider to be synonymous with effortlessness), Mihaly Csikszentimalyi states the following in an interview with *Wired Magazine*: "We become involved in an activity for its own sake. The ego falls away. Time flies. Every action, movement, and thought follows inevitably from the previous one, like playing jazz" (Geirland, 2004). If we understand and regularly cultivate the stages of effort and effortless effort, effortlessness is right around the corner. Finally, keep in mind that the process of creativity belongs to everyone, regardless of circumstances. Now let's visit the Congo to see a stellar example of the interplay between the process of creativity and the realm of effortlessness.

"We become involved in an activity for its own sake. The ego falls away. Time flies. Every action, movement, and thought follows inevitably from the previous one, like playing jazz."

AN ORCHESTRA IN THE CONGO

After we've mastered a skill—and especially if we thoroughly enjoy the task—the next stage, effortlessness, holds tremendous and often powerful potential and can provide feelings of deep fulfillment. The following example illustrates how *anyone,* despite difficult circumstances, can dive into his/her core of effortlessness.

During an April 2012 *60 Minutes* segment, reporter Bob Simon highlighted the Kimbanguist Symphony Orchestra. This orchestra is based in the Congo, a war-torn country and home to the poorest of the poor. Here struggle is evident on nearly everyone's face. Creating a website is not the problem to be solved. Eating to stay alive, finding adequate and clean water, earning enough money just to survive—these are daily problems to solve.

In 1992, the man who would become the orchestra's leader, Armand Diangienda, lost his job as a pilot. Despite this misfortune, he had a vision: to create a symphony orchestra in Kinshasa, Congo's capital city. He started from ground zero, with little musical ability, no funding, no instruments, no practice space and, most significant, no one in the orchestra. But those obstacles did not deter him. Not only did he teach himself music but he also recruited and taught many of his fellow church members. Together they practiced in Armand's home and also repaired broken musical instruments. Performances took place in a rented warehouse (Taylor & Laguerre, 2012).

In 2010, two German filmmakers produced a documentary on Armand's story, attracting the attention of donors and garnering professional support. When *60 Minutes* filmed the orchestra half-a-world away in 2012, its cameras easily captured the absolute joy and transformation on the faces of the 200 volunteer musicians. Some played instruments; others sang. All appeared to be in a state of effortlessness. Viewers were left spellbound and in tears.

Most would agree that ongoing effort was an integral part of the orchestra members' creative process. For example, it required tremendous effort for two young brothers to simply show up to the practices. The two boys trekked on foot and traveled by bus, three hours each day, 20 miles round trip, to practice with the orchestra six days a week (Taylor & Laguerre, 2012). The daily trek built an ingrained neural network (a new habit) that probably helped the boys to experience the arduous task as more effortless than not. However, what followed on

"When '60 Minutes' filmed the orchestra half a world away in 2012, its cameras easily captured the absolute joy and transformation on the faces of 200 volunteer musicians."

the heels of their determination and effort was their utter freedom through singing. One could see sheer joy in their faces; their contributions to the orchestra allowed them to enter into a process of creativity and ultimately experience the deep satisfaction of effortlessness.

Members of the Kimbanguist Symphony Orchestra sing or play music; your vehicle will likely be different. However, it does not matter if you're in the Congo playing a refurbished French horn or sitting in your living room tinkering on a website; the process of creativity remains the same. Each of us has the capability to experience our inherent state of effortlessness. You will feel incredibly good after being immersed in your unique flow, which can occur equally through a variety of vehicles—whether writing a stage play or creating a recipe, whether building an engine or cleaning out drawers. Ideally, the process of creativity becomes an ingrained habit so that you can consciously access your flow on a regular basis.

An important aspect is to be ever mindful that you are in effort rather than struggle. Once you are in the stage of effort, you can expect effort and effortless effort to seesaw. As mentioned previously, you may spend an undetermined period of time between effort and effortless effort. However, remaining in effortless effort will ultimately allow you to slip into effortlessness. Yet, even when the process of creativity becomes a habit, it will still take daily practice. We will always be students of the process of creativity.

"… it does not matter if you're in the Congo playing a refurbished French horn or sitting in your living room tinkering on a website; the process of creativity remains the same. Each of us has the capability to experience our inherent state of effortlessness."

8

perfect & on time

Normal perfectionistic standards are less about achieving

perfectionism and more about striving for excellence.

CHAPTER EIGHT

PERFECTIONISM AND PROCRASTINATION

For some, "perfectionism" and "procrastination" are words that generate the laughter of deep recognition (you know who you are!). Others cringe when recalling the crippling effects of a previous bout of perfectionism or procrastination, especially when trying to complete a project. From working with students and personal experience, I know that these two behaviors, when left unmonitored, can activate struggle and wreak absolute havoc on the process of creativity.

Years of observation have shown me that perfectionism and procrastination walk hand in hand as a finely woven interplay of our humanness and brain chemistry. Yet we tend to focus on procrastination as a negative behavior, a character flaw, while praising perfectionism. Based on my research, procrastination *and* perfectionism both have the power to hold us hostage when we are trying to start or continue an endeavor.

Once again, my students have shown me the faces of these pesky traits. At the beginning of each semester, I guide students through the following exercise: acknowledge and write three of your strengths and three of your weaknesses. Over the years, a consistent pattern has emerged from this activity. Regardless of age, nationality, or gender, many students readily admit to being perfectionists while others profess to the habit of ongoing procrastination. Some admit to both. Although everyone has a good laugh, without a teaching intervention, these traits tend to show up as soon as the first assignment is due.

In addition to my direct experience with students, the following research statistic has shed additional light: according

"… I know that these two behaviors, when left unmonitored, can activate struggle and wreak absolute havoc on the process of creativity."

to a 2007 meta-analysis, "procrastination plagues a whopping 80 to 95 percent of college students ..." (Gura, 2008, p. 26). Indeed, procrastination runs rampant among students. In my opinion, everyone is affected by procrastination. But what most educators do not understand is that procrastination need not be viewed as a character flaw but rather as a psychological result of complex brain functions. And surprise, surprise ... the same holds true for perfectionism.

"The assignment seemed simple enough to me—but then I had been designing and sketching logos for years! Sixty sketches might take me an hour. However, for my students, in spite of the fact that I had reviewed the assignment during class, the task proved daunting."

For instance, in the past, I would assign 60 logo sketches due at the beginning of the next day's class. The assignment seemed simple enough to me—but then I had been designing and sketching logos for years! Sixty sketches might take me an hour. However, for my students, in spite of the fact that I had reviewed the assignment during class, the task proved daunting. Why? Their brains were going crazy. They did not have enough initial information, instruction, or practice to even begin their sketches. The results? While trying to tackle their homework assignment, they were uncertain what to do or how to do it. Eventually, I realized that an overwhelming task causes the brain to respond with the behaviors of perfectionism and procrastination.

If a student is uncertain about what is expected, s/he will not have enough confidence to fulfill the homework assignment. Dr. Timothy Pychyl, faculty member of the Department of Psychology at Carlton University and frequent blogger for *Psychology Today*, states that the major correlate of procrastination is, simply put, task uncertainty (Pychyl, 2009). Further, when a learner feels out of control or highly controlled, "the only learning possible involves rote memorization or learning of simple skills" (Howard, 2006, p. 512). The only problem solving or creativity possible "is based on habits, instincts, or other already learned routinized behaviors" (Howard, 2006, p. 512). As a result of task uncertainty, the brain experiences a cascade of reactions. The student will stress. Struggle will arise. The brain will toggle into the fight, flight, or freeze mode. The high beta brainwave state will kick into gear and, with it, an inability to use the problem-solving cerebral cortex. In short, students will be unable to think clearly. At this point, the student experiences discomfort, which translates to thoughts that the assignment is too big. All of these reactions overwhelm the student and procrastination sets in. But, in actuality, the problem has just begun.

"We love our perfect students. Though we support excellence, we may unwittingly be contributing to unchecked perfectionism."

CROSSING THE T'S AND DOTTING THE I'S OF PERFECTIONISM

Let's admit it. Educators love to love those students who turn in assignments perfectly and on time. We show off this perfect work to other educators and to other students. We love our perfect students. Though we support excellence, we may unwittingly be contributing to unchecked perfectionism. This is a problem. Why?

Perfectionism is generally seen as "striving for flawlessness" (Flett & Hewitt, 2002, p. 5). Though researchers have a slightly different view and definition of perfectionism, psychologist D. E. Hamachek has theorized that perfectionism becomes a problem when it moves from normal to neurotic (Hamachek, 1978). In addition, neuroscientists know perfectionism causes the brain to develop "excessive levels of serotonin that are associated with obsessiveness, including obsession with perfection" (Howard, 2006, p. 761). From a neuroscientfic perspective, although serotonin is a neurotransmitter linked to happiness, too much of it causes restlessness, a fast heartbeat, and rapid changes in blood pressure. Nonetheless, regardless of the psychological or scientific perspectives, from my perspective, unchecked perfectionism will quickly knock us out of our process of creativity.

But when is perfectionism unchecked? Using psychological terms, Hamachek describes perfectionism as two types: normal or neurotic (Hamachek, 1978). According to Hamachek's analysis, normal perfectionism involves high personal expectations—but with an allowance for flexibility. Hamachek further states that normal perfectionists "… are better able to establish performance boundaries that take into account both their limitations and strengths. In this way, success is more possible because self expectations are both more reasonable and realistic" (Hamachek, 1978). When we display normal perfectionism, we've produced the work to the best of our ability. We're happy with the outcome of the project.

From my perspective, normal perfectionistic standards are less about achieving perfectionism and more about striving for excellence. Also, the students who fall into this category demonstrate an easier time meeting deadlines because they appear to have better developed time-management and goal-setting skills. In my opinion, normal perfectionism is not a problem. On the other hand, neurotic perfectionism

"From my perspective, normal perfectionistic standards are less about achieving perfectionism and more about striving for excellence."

certainly seems to be unchecked perfectionism and a problem. Neurotic perfectionists demand of themselves "a higher level of performance than it is usually possible to attain; and this, of course, severely reduces their possibilities for feeling good about themselves" (Hamachek, 1978).

As an early proponent of working with perfectionism in children, W. Hugh Missildine wrote, "Our clinical work with children clearly indicates that this continual self-belittlement—rather than a desire to master the environment—is the real driving force behind the perfectionist's unending efforts" (Missildine, 1963, p. 83). For many, "Perfectionism at work tends to herald that paralyzed state of all or nothing" (Weber, 2007). Therefore, neurotic perfectionism is not about striving for excellence but rather a behavior driven by a constantly harping internal voice making unreasonable demands. To say this is problematic may be an understatement.

My students often reveal their unchecked perfectionism by making demeaning and overly critical comments about their work. Such comments signal an overall lack of self-confidence. To compensate for their insecurity, students will overdo, over design, overwork, or overproduce the project at hand. Theirs is an all-or-nothing approach. They either meet the deadline with an overabundance of material or completely miss the deadline, paralyzed by neurotic perfectionism. Again ... big problem.

In my opinion, one of the main obstacles to the process of creativity is neurotic perfectionism. And ... think about it, we probably all hear some version of this belittling, critical inner voice. Most of us swing along the continuum between

"My students often reveal their unchecked perfectionism by making demeaning and overly critical comments about their work. Such comments signal an overall lack of self-confidence."

normal and neurotic perfectionism, depending upon the task at hand. Being aware of our tendencies towards perfectionism is the first step towards preventing us from swinging wildly and counterproductively along this continuum.

OVERCOMING UNCHECKED PERFECTIONISM AND PROCRASTINATION

"After a series of several short exercises, coupled with feedback and guidance from me and other classmates, their confidence level rises."

So how do we overcome unchecked perfectionism and procrastination? In the case of my students, to transcend the *all or nothing* of perfectionism, they must first receive enough instruction—and put in enough time and effort learning *how* to produce a logo—before they start sketching. After they've thoroughly researched and discussed why certain logos work and others don't, only then are they given the go-ahead for their first set of in-class sketches. As they attempt to enter into their process of creativity, we discuss the brain functions and the need to remain calm. After a series of several short exercises, coupled with feedback and guidance from me and other classmates, their confidence level rises. As a result, when it's time to produce their homework assignment, the unchecked perfectionism is tempered. In this way they tend to avoid the ill effects of unchecked procrastination. After working on the exercises and getting a handle on the process of creativity, successfully solving the problem at hand becomes more effortless than not.

But how does this translate to our own unique projects and entering into the process of creativity? We need to be aware that anyone with a tendency towards perfectionism will likely struggle and perhaps *procrastinate* when beginning a project or

endeavor—especially *if* they don't have enough instruction.
In summary, it's a good idea to ask two questions before
beginning a new endeavor. Do I know the necessary steps to
take? Do I feel confident enough to start the project? Even a
normal perfectionist may not understand what they are doing
before starting a project (i.e., what the process entails) and this
can lead them to procrastinate. On the other hand, a neurotic
perfectionist may know exactly what to do but may lack the
necessary confidence to get started and follow through. However,
there is some good news about overcoming procrastination.

THE HAPPY NEUROTRANSMITTER

Up to now, we've discussed the negative reactions of the brain.
However, the brain also has positive functions that try to promote
happiness and, even better, help to overcome procrastination.
On a related note, Barry Richmond of the National Institute
of Mental Health has determined that "the gene controlling
the production of dopamine receptors is associated with
procrastination" (Howard, 2006, p. 761). In 1995, psychologist
Richard Depue found that the neurotransmitter dopamine was
linked to happiness. Not only is dopamine linked to happiness
but it also seems that its steady flow allows us to sense an
upcoming reward (Howard, 2006). Yet, if we place that reward
too far in the future, dopamine cannot sense the potential reward
(Pilcher, 2004). This simple brain function is partly responsible
for our procrastination when a deadline looms too far in the
future. The dopamine cannot sense the upcoming reward,

*"... it's a good idea to
ask two questions before
beginning a new endeavor.
Do I know the necessary
steps to take? Do I feel
confident enough to start
the project?"*

whatever it may be. So now the question becomes: how do we reward ourselves to avoid falling into procrastination?

Every year, I face a daunting project: getting my taxes ready for my accountant. Having struggled through this process in the past, I see that both perfectionism and procrastination can come into play. My prior experience makes me aware of potential struggle; indeed, all the accompanying reactive brain functions are right around the corner, just waiting for me to slip and slide. But the brain has also taught me a few tricks.

Before beginning my taxes, I make a detailed list of all the many, many tasks—then separate those tasks into small doable actions. Some actions are as simple as making a call to set up an appointment with my accountant. Others take longer (but no more than an hour), such as categorizing receipts from the previous year. The trick is to make sure each action takes only a short time to accomplish, between one minute and one hour.

In addition to the small doable tasks, my other trick is to accompany a completed task with a tiny reward. My "reward system" consists of moving shiny pebbles from one bowl to another after I have finished a task. After a few hours, and scratching a number of items off my list, the "task" bowl is full of shiny objects and my project is complete. Now … this system may sound simplistic but each new pebble provides me a delightful moment of glee. In turn, my dopamine receptors sense these little moments of happiness and, therefore, keep me feeling enthused. These seemingly simple steps not only send a "reward" signal to my brain but also help me maintain momentum towards achieving my goal. By the end of the weekend, taxes are done and

"The trick is to make sure each action takes only a short time to accomplish, between one minute and one hour. In addition to the small doable tasks, my other trick is to accompany a completed task with a tiny reward."

the project has been more effortless than not. When working on any project or endeavor, particularly if it is large with many steps, try to find a tiny reward that will activate your dopamine. The result? More than likely, you won't procrastinate!

YOUR PROBLEM TO SOLVE

Depending upon the task at hand, we all experience behavioral swings up and down the continuum of procrastination and perfectionism. Unchecked perfectionism may cause us to overproduce and still not feel satisfied with our output. Unchecked perfectionism likes to nip at one's brain, reinforcing the voice of self-judgment: do I really have anything of value to say, to do, or to offer? Likewise, procrastination is oftentimes the result of task uncertainty; it is this uncertainty that causes one to feel out of control. Finally, making sure that the steps to complete a project are small—and that each step is rewarded—can help keep procrastination and perfectionism at bay.

"Finally, making sure that the steps to complete a project are small—and that each step is rewarded—can help keep procrastination and perfectionism at bay."

9

CRAWLING DOWN
a few rabbit holes

*There are many instances in history when theories seemed
unquantifiable (according to the science of that particular era)
only to be proved valid at a later time.*

CHAPTER NINE

THE MIND WORKING WITH THE BRAIN

We've arrived! And now we're ready to weave the concept of Thuse or, more accurately, the Mind of Thuse, into the process of creativity. In previous chapters, we diligently explored how the brain blocks us from the process of creativity by manufacturing emotions and memories, often resulting in struggle. We also acquired an understanding of how effort allows us to slip into the process of creativity—and can lead us into the stage of effortless effort. With practice, we may learn to rely upon the process of creativity to live our daily lives with less stress—by toggling between effort and effortless effort. From there, we may more easily experience effortlessness and, ultimately, the Mind of Thuse.

While we've already referenced the word *Thuse* in earlier chapters and will explore the term more thoroughly in a later chapter, right now let's look more specifically at what is meant by the expression *Mind of Thuse*. First, let us make a distinction between the mind and the brain. Scientists can dissect, analyze, measure, and document brain functions with tangible results; however, scientists have been unable to pinpoint or quantify the mind. As a result, the study of the mind has been relegated to such disciplines as philosophy and psychology. Finally, it is a common misconception that the mind and the brain are one and the same. In my opinion, they are not.

While the Mind of Thuse includes the body and brain, it actually encompasses infinitely more—guiding us towards something mysterious and unquantifiable. The mystery may lie behind what physicists have been theorizing for years: our

"With practice, we may learn to rely upon the process of creativity to live our daily lives with less stress—by toggling between effort and effortless effort."

cosmos could consist of an underlying fabric of vibrating strings. In addition, this Mind of Thuse might be viewed as a unique aspect of our humanness that is able to consciously acknowledge and access something larger—an infinite mind-set. In my opinion, the Mind of Thuse is the body/brain's awareness of our interconnectedness with this infinite mind-set, this fabric of vibrating strings. Yes … you read that right.

"… this Mind of Thuse might be viewed as a unique aspect of our humanness that is able to consciously acknowledge and access something larger—an infinite mind-set."

The process of creativity allows for the brain to purposefully connect to the Mind of Thuse. When thriving within the Mind of Thuse, one naturally and consciously understands that the vibrating outer world is the direct result of our vibrating inner world. What we see outside of ourselves mirrors what we are thinking, feeling, vibrating inside. When we exist within this infinite nature, questions become less relevant because we are living within the answer. This is the ultimate form of effortlessness.

However, to apply effortlessness within our daily lives takes the practice of keeping the brain calm. When the brain is calm we can cultivate the ability to "see" and "observe" reactive activity with the brain. Developing a keen awareness of and sensitivity to how we react emotionally in any given situation is a type of training—training that helps us avoid being governed by automatic, and sometimes adverse, reactions. By understanding the fine balance between accessing the mind and being controlled by the reactions of the chemical brain, we begin to develop the ability to recognize an inner voice or "knowingness." The process of creativity puts the beauty of inner knowing—sometimes referred to as "an awakened mind"—at our fingertips.

FOR THE LOVE OF SCIENCE

Now let's make believe for a few minutes … and step into the shoes of a scientist. From a scientific standpoint, the concept of the Mind of Thuse might be viewed as unquantifiable and, therefore, esoteric and philosophical because science is based on theories that are ultimately proved (or disproved) as a result of substantive research and experimentation. Scientists are trained to prove their theories by experiments that can be replicated. If proof does not exist, the theory may be viewed as interesting philosophy, but philosophy nonetheless.

But there are many instances in history when theories seemed unquantifiable (according to the science of that particular era) only to be proved valid at a later time. For example, when Christopher Columbus lived, traditional scientific thought considered the world to be flat. Few would accept the idea that the world was, in fact, round. And … if anyone dared to speak of the world being round, he was considered a philosopher at best and a heretic at worst. Today, we know and accept that the earth is round.

Similarly, 150 years ago the Scottish mathematical physicist James Clerk Maxwell wrote an equation that helped to predict electromagnetic waves (Maxwell, 2012). Again, the thought at the time was that these invisible waves did not exist. Today, however, the concept of electromagnetism is commonplace; as a result of electromagnetic waves, we can listen to the radio and talk on cell phones.

These are just two examples demonstrating that even though physical phenomena cannot always be readily seen or

"Similarly, 150 years ago the Scottish mathematical physicist James Clerk Maxwell wrote an equation that helped to predict electromagnetic waves. Again, the thought at the time was that these invisible waves did not exist."

perceived, that does not necessarily mean they do not exist. Currently, there are some quantum physicists who seem to be in a similar situation to those of the scientists during the days of Columbus and Maxwell. From a historical perspective, then, humankind has not always been able to perceive physical reality as it actually is. In other words, *if people cannot see what is right in front of them, they have a tendency to believe that it does not exist.*

"From an historical perspective, then, humankind has not always been able to perceive physical reality as it actually is."

NOW YOU SEE IT. NOW YOU DON'T!

The infinitesimal world of mystery that currently challenges physicists is the quantum world. Basically, quantum mechanics deals with physical reality at the subatomic level and centers around theories such as Heisenberg's uncertainty principle and wave-particle duality. Within quantum mechanics, mathematical tools can predict outcomes of experiments with impeccable accuracy. Theoretical physicist Richard Feynman once said, "I think I can safely say that nobody understands quantum mechanics" (Hey & Walters, 2003).

Few would argue that quantum mechanics is a highly complex, and often baffling, science; however, let's deal at present only with the philosophical implications. Even highly controlled laboratory experiments may not provide a complete understanding of the underlying processes (Aczel, 2003). No one can actually pinpoint the quantum world because it is both here and there. Now you see it. Now you don't. On what precise physical levels does the quantum world exist?

In the same way, no one can actually pinpoint the workings of the mind. Furthermore, no mathematical equation is available to prove or disprove its existence. Yet the renowned neuroscientist Richie Davidson is paving the way with impressive research. During an interview with Davidson for an article titled "Taking Measure of the Mind," Barry Boyce reports that the mind may not be so "easily defined and delineated as the brain" (Boyce, 2012).

Davidson's research, primarily targeting affective disorders such as anxiety and depression, has shown that when the mind trains the brain, beneficial effects may be measured (Boyce, 2012). Thank you, Richie Davidson, for your much-needed research. In terms of the process of creativity, from my perspective, certain scientific theories may have given us a glimpse of the infinite and, at the same time, infinitesimal Mind. Since I'm going out on a limb anyway to make a few points, might as well dive a little deeper into quantum mechanics.

"Searching for a theory that unifies general relativity with quantum mechanics, scientists have been in a race to find the "basic, fundamental, indivisible, constituents making up everything in the world around us."

STRING THEORY AND M THEORY

Searching for a theory that unifies general relativity with quantum mechanics, scientists have been in a race to find the "basic, fundamental, indivisible, constituents making up everything in the world around us" (TEDtalksDirector, 2008). Not an easy task. In fact, Einstein died before he could solve this universal riddle. The ability to write one elegant mathematical equation to explain the existence of everything has so far eluded us. Who would dare take on unifying the world of the infinitesimally small—quantum theory—with the seemingly incompatible and much larger world of relativity?

Enter stage right: string theory. String theory is the first theory to mathematically reconcile Einstein's Theory of Relativity with quantum physics (TEDtalksDirector, 2008). To grasp the concept, look at an object sitting near you—perhaps a coffee cup. What is the makeup of the cup? Clay? Yes. Paint? Yes. But when we go deep inside the clay and paint, there are countless atoms comprised of subatomic particles such as electrons, neutrons, and protons. Smaller still is the quark. Is there anything smaller than a quark? According to string theory, there certainly is.

Deep inside subatomic particles may be dancing filaments of energy that resemble vibrating strings. Just like vibrating strings on a violin or cello, these tiny strings vibrate at different frequencies and thus create patterns that, in turn, produce the different particles that make up the cosmos. If string theory is correct, these strings are the microscopic landscape of all universes (TEDtalksDirector, 2008).

Although string theory has its critics, the mere idea that our cosmos may have an underlying fabric of vibrating strings has sparked a flurry of research. In fact, research teams from across the planet continue to defend more than six separate versions of string theory.

Traditional physicists have expressed disdain for string theory partly because it cannot be proven or disproven through experiment. Just think: if the first string theory was uncomfortable for (traditional) physicists to accept, imagine six! Yet even more fascinating is the fact that the mathematical

"Although string theory has its critics, the mere idea that our cosmos may have an underlying fabric of vibrating strings has created a flurry of research."

equations supporting string theory work only if 11 different dimensions are acknowledged—six of which we cannot see nor detect. Other dimensions!! At this point, as the nonscientist, I have to chuckle at the thought of several versions of string theory attempting to explain not only the underlying substance of our universe but now also numerous dimensions. This is getting a tad messy. Even I want to tidy things up a bit.

     In an effort to unify the first five theories, a well-respected string theorist, Edward Witten of the Institute for Advanced Study, presented his thoughts at a 1994 string theory conference at the University of Southern California. On that day Witten, considered a top researcher in superstring theory, dropped a bombshell. Enter stage left: M Theory. The M theory presented by Witten became an extension of the initial five string theories. He purported that all five theories were actually describing the same concept, just seen from different perspectives. However, the neat package of M theory still did not explain the how's and why's. In fact, during an interview Witten indicated that the M stands for Magic, Mystery, or Matrix, but the letter *also* stands for Murky because the truth about M theory is quite fuzzy (PBS: NOVA Teachers, 2006). Other descriptors for the letter M have been Mother, Monster, and Membrane. If everyone is getting a shot at naming the big mystery, well then ... it's my turn! Perhaps M stands for Mind. *Perhaps the universal vibrating strings of string theory are the mysterious makeup of the infinite Mind.* Well ... at least that's my murky opinion.

"At this point, as the nonscientist, I have to chuckle at the thought of several versions of string theory attempting to explain not only the underlying substance of our universe but now also numerous dimensions."

THE MIND OF THUSE!!

WHAT THE MYSTICS HAVE SAID

Looking beyond the mystery of quantum theories, it is worth acknowledging that mystics have been involved with this realm for centuries. Mystics have based their philosophical insights, as well as countless writings and teachings, on direct personal experience. Through the eyes of mystics, who needs a mathematical equation to prove the nature of reality when they themselves are living proof? Could it be that scientists are on the edge of discovering what mystics have long surmised?

"Mystics have based their philosophical insights, as well as countless writings and teachings, on direct personal experience."

One such mystic, Georgii Ivanovich Gurdjieff (1877-1949), was a 20th century Greek-Armenian renaissance man interested in ancient knowledge. Combining areas as diverse as psychology, philosophy, science, and music, Gurdjieff resembled "... more the figure of a Zen patriarch or a Socrates than a Christian mystic ... and was considered by those who knew him simply as an incomparable 'awakener of men'" (de Salzman, 1999). Although many mystics may be cited with similar philosophies, the words of Gurdjieff have particularly resonated with me. The following is a quote from Jeffrey Werbock, published in the *Gurdjieff International Review*:

> *Gurdjieff presented us with a system of knowledge*
> *informing us that all matter and energy vibrates. Modern*
> *science has corroborated that revelation. Everything is*
> *a composition of pulsating energies vibrating across the*
> *whole spectrum of frequencies. We ourselves are just such*
> *compositions made of finer and denser energies, and*
> *by actively listening to the microtones on inner octaves,*

we may experience a relationship with the finer levels of energies that are an integral part of our own being. Sensing the presence of another level of energy, we find that the higher is accessible through the inner. (Werbock, 2004)

With this explanation, we might ask: what are these inner microtones and how do we attune ourselves to them? Could perhaps hearing and responding to these microtones be incomprehensible to the brain, yet powerfully accessible to the mind?

    While I may not know the exact nature of the microtones, perhaps they are an "inner knowing" that results from "hearing" the underlying fabric of vibrating strings. Consider this: with various strings vibrating inside of every particle in the universe, could our connection with the expanded mind "hear" other vibrating strings—regardless of their location? If these internal vibrating strings do, in fact, exist, then is our internal physical reality more expansive than that perceived and controlled by our limited brain? Could this attuned nature be the basis for events such as synchronicity, miracles, luck, and coincidence?

    On the flip side, could our focus on everything that is wrong in our lives attune us to and manifest other similar and discordant vibrations? If so, would being able to hear these microtones—which would necessitate having a quiet brain and an awareness of the Mind of Thuse—help us to *thrive* in a daily experience of the miraculous and unexpected? Perhaps then the

"If these internal vibrating strings do, in fact, exist, then is our internal physical reality more expansive than that perceived and controlled by our limited brain?"

result would be that the miraculous just becomes commonplace. Hang on. We're almost there.

EXPERIMENTS BY ERNST CHLADNI

Let's move now from the scientific quantum world and that of esoteric mysticism into the tangible reality we can actually see and experience with our senses. We begin by observing the work of German physicist, naturalist, and musician Ernst F. F. Chladni (1756-1827). Chladni performed a series of experiments using glass plates covered with fine sand. He then stroked the glass plates with a violin bow. The friction of the bow against the edge of the plate made the glass "sing" much like when you lightly glide a finger around the wet rim of a crystal glass. He discovered that particular patterns in the sand occurred depending upon the pitch of the vibration created by the action of the bow (Lauterwasser, 2006).

"Perhaps then the result would be that the miraculous just becomes commonplace."

In much the same way that Chladni viewed differing frequencies etched in the sand as unique images, we can begin to understand how we cause our own reality—through the effects of our conscious thoughts and intentions, as well as our unconscious thoughts. In the case of Chladni's experiments, the cause of the vibration was the stroke of a violin bow. The effect of the vibration was the manipulation of the sand—resulting in the image of a pattern caused by that vibration.

Perhaps this cause-and-effect relationship is one reason why it is so important to supplant the reactive brain with the more positive aspects of the mind. Much like the patterns of sand, we create our own "snapshots of vibration." These snapshots reflect our day-to-day experiences. What situations and experiences are we knowingly or unknowingly creating with our unique vibrations?

THE RESEARCH OF MASARU EMOTO

To answer the previous question, we turn to Japanese author and entrepreneur Masaru Emoto, author of *The New York Times* best seller *The Hidden Messages In Water,* whose experiments with the molecular structure of water have produced results reminiscent of Chladni's sand etchings. Emoto took the world by storm with his claim that the crystalline structure of water changes according to environmental factors—factors such as words, prayers, and music.

"... this cause and effect relationship is one reason why it is so important to supplant the reactive brain with the more positive aspects of the mind."

Emoto's research was sparked by his keen interest in water. One day, while reading a book, the following statement caught his eye: "No two snow crystals are exactly the same" (Emoto, 2001, p. xx). From this seemingly inconsequential fact, it dawned on Emoto that if he froze water, surely each crystal would be unique. Two months of experimentation confirmed that this was true.

His first photograph was of a "beautiful hexagonal crystal" (Emoto, 2001, p. xxi). Emoto then began experimenting with many different kinds of water—from Tokyo's tap water to pure water from natural springs. Here comes the fascinating part. The tap water contained no complete crystals. On the other hand, all natural pure water—from glaciers to spring water—had beautifully formed crystalline structures.

He went on to experiment with music, playing the melodies of Beethoven, Mozart, and Chopin next to water. The results? Beethoven's Pastoral Symphony, with its bright and clear tones, resulted in beautiful, well-formed crystals. Mozart's 40th Symphony, a graceful prayer to beauty, created crystals that were delicate and elegant. And the crystals formed by exposure to Chopin's Etude in E, Op. 10, No. 3, surprised Emoto with their lovely detail.

"Next, he wrapped bottles of water with pieces of paper containing written words such as love, gratitude, and fool. The results continued to be astounding. One of the most beautiful six-pointed crystals was formed by the words love and gratitude."

In contrast, water placed next to the music of "violent heavy metal" produced "fragmented and malformed crystals" (Emoto, 2001, p. xxiv). Emoto's experimentation did not stop there. Next, he wrapped bottles of water with pieces of paper containing written words such as *love, gratitude,* and *fool.* The results continued to be astounding. One of the most beautiful six-pointed crystals was formed by the words love and gratitude. The word fool created a fragmented crystal, much like the heavy metal music had done.

After reading Emoto's book, I felt a veil had been lifted; I saw our individual contributions to these vibrations. The water crystals are similar to Chladni's unique images etched in the sand. Both examples illustrate how conscious or unconscious intentions generate cause and effect in our physical world. From these results, I began to consider how these experiments reinforced my personal perspective on why what we do, say, or think is so very, very, very important. Similar to the images etched in the sand and the frozen water crystals, we, too, are vibratory snapshots changing moment by moment. And the types of changes that we experience depend almost exclusively on our input, similar to Emoto's environmental factors.

But how does all this science and philosophy affect our process of creativity? By understanding the importance of how we cultivate and feed our brains—with thoughts and feelings that are more calm and positive than not—we are able to build a foundation for the process of creativity. Once we really "get" and apply this concept, we leave behind struggle and are able to activate the process of creativity in our daily lives through practice, practice, and more practice. As a result, we pave a pathway that actively engages the toggle between effort and effortless effort. With that, we are able to experience effortlessness more easily and stand ready at the doorway of the Mind of Thuse. But we're not done yet. In fact, we're just beginning.

"Similar to the images etched in the sand and the frozen water crystals, we, too, are vibratory snapshots changing moment by moment."

10

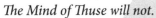

EXPLORING

effortlessness times three

I know that the brain is a trickster. The Mind of Thuse is not. The brain will convince us of the necessity to struggle. The Mind of Thuse will not.

CHAPTER TEN

THE FIRST LEVEL OF EFFORTLESSNESS

Now that we've gone down a few rabbit holes, from quantum mechanics to the philosophy of mystics, from sand etchings to water crystals, we're back! Armed with new information, it's time to weave the threads of these principles into the process of creativity—which will take us to effortlessness and finally into the Mind of Thuse. Hang on! We're about to dig up our own rabbit hole!

Until now we've been dealing with effortlessness as a general concept. It's time to focus on specifics. First and foremost, the state of effortlessness is actually comprised of three levels. The first level of effortlessness, for the most part, can be described as *goal oriented with predictable outcomes.* Within this first level, we may be writing a short story, cleaning out a closet, or repairing a car engine. While involved in these projects, we begin to experience an effortlessness accompanied by boundless energy and timelessness that allows us to focus so intently on the endeavor or task at hand that nothing else seems to exist. This effortless moment then becomes larger, more mysterious, and more all encompassing than the task at hand because, as you may recall, this is the moment when the painter allows the painting to paint itself. As we tap into this level of effortlessness, we begin to connect with the underlying fabric of the universe: that is, the Mind of Thuse.

THE SECOND LEVEL OF EFFORTLESSNESS

Within the second level of effortlessness, one begins to *manifest desired outcomes,* ranging from the fulfillment of specific

"Armed with new information, it's time to weave the threads of these principles into the process of creativity."

immediate needs to long-term goals. To illustrate, let's look back to the time Jane needed an extra $220 for her car repair. Remember how the additional money "magically" showed up within a couple of days and she was able to pay for that repair? How exactly did that money show up? At the time, Jane only had $40 in her account, with no income in sight. Haven't we all experienced this "magical" sort of surprise at some point in our lives? Various cultures refer to these surprises as miracles, coincidence, or even luck. But in my opinion, there is an explanation that lies behind these mysterious descriptors. So, let's head back to the work of Emoto and his water crystals. Hang on to that shovel!

According to Emoto's experiments, water crystals replicate the vibration of their immediate environment. That is, vibrations actually change the physical nature of the water. If surrounded by a harmonious environment, the water creates beautifully harmonious crystalline structures. In contrast, if the vibrations of the surroundings are discordant, then distorted crystals will be the result.

Now, because our bodies are also primarily made up of water, what if, hypothetically, we were able to isolate and freeze a sample of water from our own bodies? In the same manner as Emoto's water crystals, what might these snapshots reveal? Would our water crystals replicate our immediate environment—our thoughts and feelings? Would our crystals be harmonious or distorted crystalline structures? Further, how do struggle and stress affect the structure of our crystals? Let's dig deeper.

"Now, because our bodies are also primarily made up of water, what if, hypothetically we were able to isolate and freeze a sample of water from our own bodies? In the same manner as Emoto's water crystals, what might these snapshots reveal?"

As previously explained, Chladni's work created sound images—snapshots of vibrations—made in the sand by a violin bow stroking the edge of a plate. Our thoughts, feelings, and environment are just like the violin bow. Our body and brain are just like the plate stroked by that violin bow. The sound that produced the etching in the sand is just like our vibration. So ... now let's think about that. What is the snapshot of our vibration?

Perhaps the snapshot of our vibration is a moment-by-moment reflection of our lives. In other words, the vibrations from our thoughts, feelings, and environment, whether harmonious or distorted, will produce our reality. What we see right in front of us is *an ongoing snapshot of our vibration.* To illustrate this concept, let's look at two examples of different levels of vibration concerning abundance.

The first story comes from a student, Tammie. One day after class, Tammie mentioned to me that she had participated in a few abundance techniques earlier in the week. Now ... keep in mind, although Tammie was open to this type of work, a community college setting does not quite lend itself to such discussions. However, there we were, as she professed the following: shortly after completing her abundance techniques, while getting into her car, she noticed a twenty-dollar bill on the ground. Upon closer inspection, she realized that it was a fifty-dollar bill. And that's not all. There were actually seven crisp, brand new fifty-dollar bills lying on the ground. To say Tammie was shocked is an understatement. Yet, in my opinion, she had made the effort to shift her vibratory rate from that of lack and struggle to one of abundance. This "miracle" was a result of

"In other words, the vibrations from our thoughts, feelings, and environment, whether harmonious or distorted, will produce our reality."

her changing her vibrations and also evidence of her changed vibratory snapshot during that place and time. Tammie's task thereafter was to remain in the vibration of abundance.

The second story comes from a dear friend, Twyla. In the process of starting a new business centered on a novel product line of children's clothing, Twyla had designed several prototypes—pieces of clothing that had generated excitement among quite a few mothers. Soon Twyla procured her first client. However, this client proved to be frustrating, in that she didn't follow through with their initial agreement or with prompt payment.

Twyla began to wonder if her vibration had attracted this type of client. Like Tammie, she took the time to engage in certain techniques—techniques centered upon value. The next day Twyla received an email from her client profusely apologizing for the delay. The client indicated a check would be in the mail, along with an additional twenty-five dollars to compensate for Twyla's inconvenience. Twyla felt certain that "doing the work"— that is, focusing on the value of her creative endeavors—had shifted her vibrational snapshot. As a result, evidence of that value (in the form of payment and compensation) showed up.

If we constantly think about and see ourselves living in ongoing struggle, we are bound to live in struggle because we are *unconsciously* manifesting that particular vibration. If we perceive our lives as a state of effortlessness, we are more likely to live in effortlessness. Tammie was shown the results of the second level of effortlessness—miraculous manifestation—by "finding" $350. In my opinion, when we thrive in effortlessness,

"If we constantly think about and see ourselves living in ongoing struggle, we are bound to live in struggle because we are unconsciously manifesting that particular vibration."

miracles are no longer the exception but instead the norm. When we comprehend the power of vibration, we begin to see why it is crucial to be cognizant of our actions, thoughts, and desires. It's up to us to recognize and integrate this simple, but not so simply accomplished, law of cause and effect.

However, equally important is recognizing when your vibration is off and being able to change it. The benefit in doing so is that you begin to consciously listen to the guidance of your inner knowing. The more conscious of the inner knowing you become and the more you attune yourself to it, the more you begin to be guided by this wisdom. The result is that the brain moves out of the driver's seat to make way for the powerful Mind of Thuse.

"When we comprehend the power of vibration, we begin to see why it is crucial to be cognizant of our actions, thoughts and desires."

THE THIRD LEVEL OF EFFORTLESSNESS

The third level of effortlessness is the Mind of Thuse, wherein lies strength, hope, and joy. The powerful Mind of Thuse … unlike the sand etchings and water crystals, we can neither see it nor touch it.

Within the third level of effortlessness, the reactive brain is at bay. One releases the experience of needs, desires, and wants. Unlike the first and second levels of effortlessness, the third level *has no goal and no desired results or expectations*. At this level, goals vanish and fulfillment of needs manifests spontaneously, almost magically. Though powerful, this level is the most difficult to trust and embrace. Why? Because it requires surrendering to something beyond the tangible, beyond our five senses.

Glimpses of the profound effects of all three levels of effortlessness were revealed to me during my travels in Nepal. In the beginning, my trek up the Himalayas was anything but effortless; struggle was the order of the day. Yet, when running down the mountain, in spite of darkness, exhaustion, and altitude sickness, I unwittingly experienced the first and second levels of effortlessness. My body felt light and strangely confident as I ran effortlessly from one rock to the next, my only intention being to arrive at the nearest lodge—alive.

But it was a few days later that I experienced a moment transcending place and time, beyond goals and expectations. That moment, occurring during a simple chat with a monk, forever changed my outlook on life. That moment is how I describe the third level of effortlessness or rather, the Mind of Thuse. And it took a mountain to show me the third level of effortlessness—the full effects of the Mind of Thuse.

Two days after running down the mountain, having recovered from altitude sickness, I decided to "get back in the saddle" and make my way up the mountain a second time. While Dawa and I were preparing to depart on that second journey, somewhere between breakfast being delayed by ten minutes and a bite of scrambled eggs, I met a monk. Beautiful maroon robes, a toothy smile, broken English, and an invitation to his monastery were all a part of our quick exchange. Yet, although I was intrigued, we made no further arrangements to connect. He went his way and I went mine. I never expected to see him again. But it seems the Mind of Thuse and the mysterious mountains were in cahoots!

"Yet, when running down the mountain, in spite of darkness, exhaustion, and altitude sickness, I unwittingly experienced the first and second levels of effortlessness."

An hour after meeting the monk, Dawa and I were on the verge of crossing a rather long bridge that swung over a rushing river. Out of the corner of my eye, I could see the monk and his crew swiftly approaching. He stopped: "You come take photographs?" Instantly the following thought arose: I don't want to take photographs. I want to pray with them. His eyes were like glittery fairy dust as he reframed his question: "Do you want to pray with us?" Astounded, I quickly accepted his invitation. Within seconds, the monk and his group flew past us to cross the bridge. To this day, I am at a loss for words when trying to describe what happened in the next few minutes. As I crossed the bridge, giant tears erupted. These were tears like no others. The tears flowed freely, openly, an acknowledgment that something was definitely up. But what was that something? I did not have a clue.

A few days later, I was back in the monk's village. Just minutes into an afternoon nap, I suddenly bolted out of bed, put on my hiking boots, and headed outside. Guess who came walking around the corner? The monk. He graciously invited me to his monastery that afternoon. I graciously accepted. Within a few hours, Dawa and I began trudging up a rather steep hill to the monk's monastery. At the top, two five-year-old soot-covered boys greeted us by blowing long, copper horns. While that sight was quite the surprise, even more shocking was my first glimpse of the monastery. I expected to see a large stone temple. Instead, the monastery was a barnlike wooden shack that looked like it might blow over in the next strong wind. But … the inside of that shack was a different story. At one end of a large room, the wall

"To this day, I am at a loss for words trying to describe what happened in the next few minutes. As I crossed the bridge, giant tears erupted. These were tears like no others."

was filled with hundreds of spiritual icons. In the middle, a very young monk scurried to feed wood into a little potbelly stove where Sherpa tea was brewing. My heart warmed as he handed me the hot delicious beverage.

The boy monks plopped themselves next to the older monk while proudly reciting chants from wide skinny books. In between sips, I tried to follow as the monk, in broken English, explained the meanings of those chants. Afterwards, the monk asked me to bow three times before the wall of icons. I quietly obliged, touching my forehead to a floor lined with a half inch of dust. Finally, the monk asked me to ring a bell a few times and light a candle with some burning incense. As beautiful as these rituals were, by the end of the afternoon I was feeling disappointed. I had expected we would meditate together and perhaps even pray.

As Dawa and I were about to depart, I asked him to ask the monk the meaning of their small prayer, or mantra—Om Mani Padme Hum. After ten minutes of animated conversation between the two, Dawa tried to translate. However, his words did not make sense. I pressed again: "I just want to know the literal translation of the words." Again Dawa spoke with the monk. Again Dawa translated. "Linda, the words are about bigness of the heart and the universe and . . ." Within the next instant, I felt a blip. Almost like a tilt. An expansion beyond my comprehension overcame me in that I knew, without a shadow of a doubt, that something in me had touched that big heart, that big universe. And that universe was not just big—it was enormous. And I, too, was just as enormous and vast as that universe.

"An expansion beyond my comprehension overcame me in that I knew, without a shadow of a doubt, that something in me had touched that big heart, that big universe."

My natural expression spilled out: "Ohhhhhhhhh!" The monk immediately smiled ear to ear, quickly clapping his hands: "That's it!! That's it!!" Stunned, all I could say was: "Danibat, danibat, danibat!" (thank you!). Two seconds later I was out the door to start my journey home—back down the steep hill, back to the lodge, back to Katmandu, back on several planes to the States, back to my life. It has taken years of writing, contemplation, and meditation to fully embrace and accept that blip. In my opinion, that blip was the Mind of Thuse—supreme effortlessness.

In my opinion, we are supposed to experience and be that blip—not just for a few moments but all day, every day. Since those days, I've developed and practiced my way of connecting to that blip, of being in that Mind of Thuse. Some days the bigness remains with me throughout the day. Other days, struggle tries to creep in and make my life hard. When this happens, I make an effort to be aware of the antics of my brain, for I know that the brain is a trickster. The Mind of Thuse is not. The brain will convince us of the necessity to struggle. The Mind of Thuse will not. *If we do not develop awareness, the brain will keep us in struggle and bar our way to The Mind of Thuse!* Herein lies the challenge.

Many individuals who practice meditation, prayer, yoga, chi gong, or any other "quieting" discipline may already be familiar with the level of effortlessness that I call the Mind of Thuse. I sure bet that serene Buddhist monk understands the Mind of Thuse! During quiet meditative moments, there is no struggle or emotions of anger, worry, guilt, or shame. Now, if this is such a great state, why can't we all get there and stay there?

"I make an effort to be aware of the antics of my brain, for I know that the brain is a trickster. The Mind of Thuse is not. The brain will convince us of the necessity to struggle. The Mind of Thuse will not."

Well, herein lies the problem. For many, there is a split between these sublime moments and the "real" moments of daily life. While one may experience expanded effortlessness and be familiar with "higher" states of consciousness while meditating or sitting quietly within temple walls, what about all the other time—when one is at work, waiting in line, paying bills, or mowing the lawn?

"My belief is that our connection to the blip, to the big cosmos, to the Mind of Thuse, is explained in large part by a conscious connection to this underlying fabric with the universe."

Stepping back into the "real world" and leaving the temple, church, or other spiritual space behind, one may automatically revert to struggling with money, career, relationship, and/or purpose in life. It is this struggle that produces the ill effects of anger, worry, guilt, and shame. What to do? Perhaps science can provide more insight into solving the problem. How to remain in the third level of effortlessness? Let's return to string theory.

STRINGS OF EFFORTLESSNESS?

What if the basic premise of string theory is correct? That is, what if the cosmos is indeed made with an underlying fabric of unified vibrating strings? Wouldn't we, too, be made up of these unified vibrating strings? I have given these questions years of thought.

My belief is that our connection to the blip, to the big cosmos, to the Mind of Thuse, is explained in large part by a conscious connection to this underlying fabric with the universe. How can this supposition help us remain within the Mind of Thuse throughout the day?

What if we lean on string theory here? Let's accept the premise that an underlying fabric of the wiggly little strings is the

118

same underlying fabric of the chair we are sitting on, of our loved ones, of landscapes halfway around the world, of the sun, moon, and distant galaxies? If we embrace this theory—that vibrating strings connect you, me, and all physical reality as one unit, one piece, one fabric—then could we not practice thinking and feeling this concept, this oneness?

When daily practicing this oneness with the Mind of Thuse, what happens when we find ourselves disconnected from the oneness? For example, when we become angry with someone? Can we then imagine seeing these wiggly strings, this unifying fabric of oneness, within not only ourselves but also the other person? If our underlying fabric of strings is indeed the same as another person's set of strings, then we have to ask: *which set of strings is angry? The strings are the same strings. So then, who is angry?*

By recalling that string theory mathematically explains our interconnected vastness, perhaps we may move our sacred experiences out of the churches, mosques, temples, (or wherever we find our spirituality), and into daily life. Given that the same strings run through such spiritual experiences as they do within our daily lives, why make such a distinction between the two? The same can be said for our emotional connectedness to one another. With this information, who is angry with whom? Who is sad about which situation? Who is happy about what? When we quit falling for the antics of the brain and move into the Mind of Thuse, life shifts. Why?

Who we are in any given moment is our vibrational snapshot. That vibrational energy will attract similar vibrational

"By recalling that string theory mathematically explains our interconnected vastness, perhaps we may move our experiences out of the churches, mosques, temples, (or wherever we find our spirituality), and into daily life."

snapshots. Live in struggle and we will attract struggle. Live in effortlessness and we will attract effortlessness. Life profoundly shifts when we finally accept responsibility for creating our vibrations and attracting like vibrations moment by moment. Our vibrations will attract what we just thought, said, or did seconds earlier. We can thrive in effortlessness, even in those areas of greatest challenge.

Can we invite effortlessness into every aspect of our lives? Can we thrive in effortlessness when functioning in the "real" world? Can we become acutely vigilant and aware of the brain's ability to highjack our best moments? Can we comprehend the apparent paradox that we are all vibrational snapshots (with individual likes and dislikes) living within a unified fabric of strings—and that, underneath it all, we are essentially the same?

When we align our intentions with vibrational energy that feels good to us, then all levels of effortlessness—including miracles, coincidence, luck, and synchronicity—begin showing up in our lives with greater frequency and eventually become commonplace. While the origin of the great cosmos and its smallest physical constituents may remain a mystery, we nevertheless have the opportunity to work consciously with the brain and the Mind of Thuse to thrive *effortlessly*—not only during our spiritual practices but also while sitting at a traffic light and running late for work!

"When we align our intentions with higher vibrational energy, then all levels of effortlessness— including miracles, coincidence, luck, and synchronicity—begin showing up in our lives with greater frequency and eventually become commonplace."

11

THE
triangle of thuse

One thing we know for sure: enthusiasm feels good. Yet Thuse is much bigger than just the emotion of enthusiasm ... working with the energy of Thuse, we become more readily able to recognize and sidestep the antics of the brain.

CHAPTER ELEVEN

REVELATION IN INDIA

After traveling to Nepal, I heard an indescribable siren call beckoning me to India. Like the Himalayas, India and her mystics have always held an inexplicable allure for me. Luckily, my meditation group in Austin was affiliated with a retreat center just a couple of hours outside of Mumbai, India.

So … in answer to the siren call, I went to India during the monsoon season of 1999. Being a goal-oriented, highly driven, type A personality, however, I needed a mission! That mission would be a six-week retreat—to rejuvenate the body, quiet the mind, and progress with my meditation. But the ancient land of India and her mystical ways had other plans in store.

After several days shaking off jet lag, exploring nearby villages, and buying Indian clothes, I started to follow the retreat center's schedule. A typical day began at 3:30 a.m. and continued with an arduous schedule until lights out at 9:00 p.m. Although my body initially rebelled at the early rising, I soon found myself eagerly waking at the prescribed time to meditate (alright, alright … sometimes I fell back to sleep while pretending to meditate!).

Following that hour of quiet, we sat silently in a dark cafeteria as ceiling fans worked overtime to keep us cool. During that time, one could hear only the swirling of fan blades and the sipping of the hottest, creamiest, sweetest chai (I still have hopes of being able to find that perfect chai in the States). At 5:30 a.m. we gathered in a temple setting to sing a lengthy Sanskrit chant. Just as we completed our final verses, the sun would begin to spill through the temple windows. These were precious moments.

"Just as we completed our final verses, the sun would begin to spill through the temple windows. These were precious moments."

After breakfast, assigned duties kept us busy until a three-hour lunch break provided an afternoon breather. During that time, we could dine, rest, or read. However, I still had my mission! I was here to relax and rejuvenate while progressing upon my meditation path. But with hours of chores each day, coupled with heat, humidity, and a demanding "supervisor," I found myself becoming quite fatigued and resentful instead. This was *certainly* not my picture of a retreat!

"Although I swore it was not the cooler temperatures that drove me into those meditation rooms, I must admit that temporarily escaping the heat and humidity was a nice perk. In hindsight, I was also calming my reactive brain."

Since little air conditioning was available, I chose to offset the rigor of my schedule by meditating in one of two cooled rooms on the grounds. Although I swore it was not the cooler temperatures that drove me into those meditation rooms, I must admit that temporarily escaping the heat and humidity was a nice perk. In hindsight, I can now see that I was also calming my reactive brain.

These meditations were joyful, sublime, and provided me much-needed rest and relaxation. Not only was I recovering from the demanding daily retreat schedule but also from my highly driven life in the States. Around the third week of these lunchtime meditations, in spite of just wanting to completely "bliss out," something interesting began to occur. The Mind of Thuse was quietly at work.

Day after day, one meditation after another, a series of mental images started to present themselves. Soon the ideas began to "draw" into a 3-D model based on an ancient philosophical writing—the Bhagavad Gita—that I was currently studying. By the end of the third week, the mysterious little 3-D model seemed to be complete. Could this revelation be an answer for how to assist my students with some of their struggles and fears, especially when they become stuck in the process of creativity? Could this model help me with my own struggles and fears?

THE RETURN

Arriving back in the States, I was eager to "test drive" the new concept with my students. When the model was drawn on the chalkboard and explained, all was silent. Truly one could have heard a pin drop. My students immediately "got" the philosophy and, naively, I thought they were forever changed!! But within minutes of everyone nodding their heads in full acknowledgment and voicing ahas, they unknowingly pitched the concept right out the window. Those ahas, as I soon discovered, were simply not enough for the model to "stick."

During the semester break I began writing a few exercises to assist my next batch of students. However, at that time, writing was not my forte. Heck! I was a painter, a graphic designer, an educator—but not a "real" writer. Yet, interestingly enough, as I followed the process of the model, words seemed to effortlessly pour forth from my fingertips onto the keyboard. At the time, I did not know why but the model seemed to be working!

THE GENESIS OF THUSE

Before introducing the model, here are a few thoughts about the word *Thuse*. At the beginning of the book, for simplicity's sake, I discussed Thuse as being effortlessness. Well ... that is just part of

" I was eager to 'test drive' the new concept with my students. When the model was drawn on the chalkboard and explained, all was silent. Truly one could have heard a pin drop. My students immediately "got" the philosophy and, naively, I thought they were forever changed!!"

the picture of Thuse. And although we've also touched the term the *Mind of Thuse*, we have not really touched on how not only the word *Thuse* evolved or what it *really* means.

When working with students or clients, I noticed how enthusiastic they became when speaking about a favorite project or endeavor. When they brought this enthusiasm to their projects, the process seemed to flow more effortlessly than not. Yet at the first sign of difficulty or obstacle, their enthusiasm often gave way to struggle. This made me wonder. Where does enthusiasm come from and how can we keep creative, passionate, enthusiastic "juices" flowing?

I've come to realize that enthusiasm is the emotion that accompanies the inception of a great idea or passion. For instance, try to recall a couple of times when you felt totally enthusiastic. In those moments, your reactive brain was most likely on hold. Did you feel as if you possessed an almost superpower energy—that you could conquer the world and nothing would get in your way? You were calm yet excited, sure of yourself, and open to possibilities. Your breathing was probably deep and full. What are these superpower moments? I see this glow of enthusiasm as the visual effect behind Thuse.

The word "enthusiasm," introduced into English during the 1600's, has a curious etymology. It comes directly from the Late Latin *enthusiasmus* and, further back, from the Greek *enthousiasmos*, meaning "divine inspiration," from *enthousiazein*, meaning "to be inspired or possessed by a god, be rapt, be in ecstasy." And finally from *entheos*, "divinely inspired, possessed by a god," from *en* "in" + *theos* "god" (Enthusiasm, n.d.). So …

"I've come to realize that enthusiasm is the emotion that accompanies the inception of a great idea or passion. For instance, try to recall a couple of times when you felt totally enthusiastic. In those moments, your reactive brain was most likely on hold."

126

are we really possessed by a god or God (depending on your view of deities) when experiencing enthusiasm? Only your personal philosophy can answer that question for you. But, one thing we know for sure: enthusiasm feels good. Yet Thuse is much bigger than just the emotion of enthusiasm.

Although Thuse and enthusiasm are interconnected, Thuse is an internal energy of a vibratory rate (think Emoto's crystals and Chladni's sound images) that also manifests externally when working with a cherished idea or passion. Remember the last time you had a great idea? Perhaps you were able to move quickly and bring that idea to fruition. Thumbs up for you! I bet your Thuse was flowing and going!

On the other hand, when I hear that someone is bored or feeling antsy about life, I simply say, "You need to get your juices flowing." By juices, I mean an enthusiasm that ignites the energy to shoo away boredom and/or that antsy feeling. Continually igniting enthusiasm fuels the energy of Thuse. In turn, the energy of Thuse boosts one's effort to become more effortless than not and ultimately leads us right into effortlessness. Thuse is what keeps us alive and vibrant, helping us remain in the process of creativity and eventually leading us into the Mind of Thuse.

Working with the energy of Thuse, we become more readily able to recognize and sidestep the antics of the brain. We do this by paying close attention to our thoughts, perceptions, words, and actions. The idea is be mindful of our vibratory rate—especially important if we know that our vibration is connected to everyone and everything—at all times! Thuse helps us to understand that whatever presents itself in our daily lives

"… one thing we know for sure: enthusiasm feels good. Yet Thuse is much bigger than just the emotion of enthusiasm … Working with the energy of Thuse, we become more readily able to recognize and sidestep the antics of the brain."

is a result of what we have been thinking, doing, and saying. Therefore, our highest priority is to be mindful of our vibratory rate so it may resonate with other similar vibrations. Tall order, I know. But it can be done. We can learn to cultivate Thuse.

Start by working on whatever project, passion, or endeavor fuels your enthusiasm. This is the first step in igniting and cultivating Thuse. Now this may be an idea sitting on the back burner, just waiting for the right time, money, support, and perhaps courage to start. That's great! As discussed in an earlier chapter, regardless of the lack of time, money, and support, start with some small aspect of that endeavor that can be broken down into even smaller doable tasks. Watch how enthusiasm starts to light a little fire of Thuse by simply doing one action a day. After you become familiar with the experience of Thuse, add it to other challenging areas of your life. One caveat, however. Thuse has to be continually cultivated. Why?

Unfortunately, we can all too easily lose our connection to Thuse. Perhaps you have been diligent about embracing your endeavor, but suddenly struggle and stress ambush your efforts. Is your brain telling you to "forget about it?" Although Thuse is always available, we are the ones who disconnect because of the reactive brain. The challenge is to keep Thuse alive and vibrant throughout an endeavor, from start to finish. Doing so will not only carry you into the process of creativity but will also lead you into effortlessness and finally into the Mind of Thuse.

"Our highest priority is to be mindful of our vibratory rate so it may resonate with other similar vibrations. Tall order, I know. But it can be done. We can learn to cultivate Thuse."

THE TRIANGLE OF THUSE

As explained earlier, the model of the Triangle of Thuse came to me during travels to India. Prior to this revelation, I had observed that many of my creative students appeared stressed. Homework was of marginal quality; many students struggled through the task of developing sketches. Because the model seemed to help me write more effortlessly, I wondered if it might also assist students with their process of creativity.

The model of the Triangle of Thuse is an aid for being able to stay connected to Thuse—so that we can fully embrace our process of creativity. The model's visual step-by-step guide enables us to deeply understand and implement the process of creativity. As a result, we ultimately move into effort, effortless effort, and effortlessness ... and finally, into the Mind of Thuse. How?

Well ... let's start with a visual (see illustration 1-A). The model is an upside-down triangle consisting of an Outer and Inner Triangle that forms a six-pointed star at the top. At this time, the important point to remember is that the Triangle of Thuse is all about *balance.*

The Outer Triangle has three sides that represent emotions and the state of one's brain (calm or reactive). The three outer sides of the Outer Triangle are based on ancient Hindu philosophy. This philosophy purports that three "attitudes" or gunas—sattva, rajas, and tamas—are found in varying degrees of concentration and combination within each individual's personality (Jayaram, n.d.). The first of the three gunas or attitudes, sattva, is all about the continuum of happiness. The

"... I had observed that many of my creative students appeared stressed."

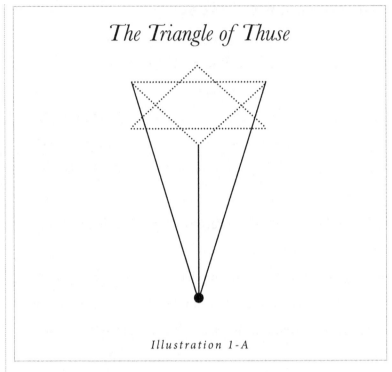

The Triangle of Thuse

Illustration 1-A

"The model of the Triangle of Thuse is an aid for being able to stay connected to Thuse—so that we can fully embrace our process of creativity."

second, rajas, is about action or activity. And finally, tamas can be compared to the "thistle brain"—when one is caught in struggle. So if we are more rajastic in nature, we stay way too busy; if we're sattvic, we're constantly striving for the next thing to make us happy; and finally, if we're tamasic in nature, life is full of struggle.

While the Hindu concept wants us to transcend these attitudes, I've adapted the philosophy to include that of balance. That is, the three sides of the Outer Triangle represent balanced aspects of the gunas—to be used as a self-reflective measurement to gauge one's own attitudes. Let's dig down a little deeper now while I describe the relevance of these attitudes, or gunas.

SATTVA: CONSCIOUSLY STRIVING

Hindu philosophy says that if we are more sattvic in nature, then we consciously strive to remain happy, balanced, calm, alert, thoughtful, and positive. Sattva also suggests equilibrium and a more or less satisfying experience of ease, mastery, and harmony. Yet, the important point to remember is that sattva is based on "striving to be happy" (Guna, 2009).

With "too much sattva" individuals may feel a need to seek out the next "thing" that will "make" them happy. We've all experienced this state: if only I can have this or do that, then I'll be happy!! Yet, the happy effects of having this or that may only last for a short time—perhaps a minute, a day, a week, a year, even ten years, and then it's back to seeking out our next bit of happiness.

Being in a balanced state of sattva is a very important attitude because it can lift us out of negative thinking into more positive moments. We experience the best of sattva when our happiness is not based on an external person, place, situation, or thing. Rather, our happiness derives from thriving in the Mind of Thuse; that is truly the best of sattva.

Now, looking at this attitude through a Western lens, let's replace sattva with a new name: *Sazy*. One definition of *Sazy* listed in the online Urban Dictionary is: "If something is incredibly awesome, yet relaxed. A zen state of being similar in idea to being bitchin'" (Sazy, 2009). Rather than seeking out something external to make you happy, you are happy simply because you are in a balanced state of Sazy.

"Sattva also suggests equilibrium and a more or less satisfying experience of ease, mastery, and harmony. Yet, the important point to remember is that sattva is based on 'striving to be happy.'"

RAJAS: FRANTIC ACTION

Second in the lineup is the state of rajas. "Rajas is the force that creates desires for acquiring new things and fears for losing something that one has" (Guna, 2009). If we are rajastic in nature, then we tend to busy ourselves with endless activity. This type of action can easily trigger struggle because we want to achieve something that will make us happy *now*. With too much rajas, we push ourselves with endless activities, goals, and expectations based on getting the "thing" that will make us happy. Yet, once that thing is acquired, we'll spend a lot of energy trying not to lose it. Exhausting!!

"With too much rajas, we push ourselves with endless activities, goals, and expectations based on getting the 'thing' that will make us happy."

Now imagine manifesting all that will meet your needs without feeling afraid that you will "lose" in any way. Objects, people, and events move into your life and, at a later time, may move out of your life—without your grasping or being in constant dread of losing them. You are able to enjoy all life has to offer without forming rigid attachments or creating unrealistic expectations. With a balance of rajas energy we *calmly* move in natural rhythm to achieve our objectives rather than operating from a position of desperation.

Once the Triangle of Thuse is understood and utilized, the covetous nature of rajas diminishes. Instead, we use rajas to fuel effort with small steps that alleviate struggle. Because rajas is at its best when action is balanced and incremental, let's pass it through the Western lens with the name *Rawkin'*, shortened to Rawk. *Rawkin'* is just another word used to describe something that appeals to you in the same way as the word *rockin'* (Rawkin', 2008).

With Rawk we learn to take baby steps when starting a new project or endeavor and, as a result, tolerate risk more easily. With Rawk, we are able to maintain effort while avoiding struggle; we are able to stay balanced in the process of creativity. Now are you ready to meet the biggest roadblock in town? That would be tamas.

TAMAS: HEAVINESS AND INERTIA

The final character in the personality roundup is tamas. If we are too tamasic in nature, there is a tendency towards heaviness or "inertia" (Guna, 2009). We lose our connection to Thuse when tamas keeps us immobilized with unconscious and subconscious behaviors—such as accepting lack, defeat, or hopelessness. With these attitudes, despondency and struggle are here to stay. Finally, if an individual is unable to reach and teach the brain's reactive nature through consistent effort, then the need to escape from struggle may result in addictions and self-destructive behaviors.

Yet, I have a little secret about tamas. The state of tamas is indeed a *lie*. *Tamas is the ongoing lie of the reactive brain that convinces us we are stuck!* Nothing, nothing, nothing could be further from the truth. There is no positive aspect to tamas. The more positive aspects of Rawk and Sazy keep tamas in balance.

The main culprit keeping us stuck in tamas is an ongoing threat to our beliefs and perceptions that we might lose "something" as a result of taking action. In tamas we can't move forward. We can't move backwards. We're stuck! Our Thuse is nowhere to be found. As a result of being stuck, a host of thoughts will mumble and churn, triggering an ongoing chemical output in the brain

"Once the Triangle of Thuse is understood and utilized, the covetous nature of rajas diminishes. Instead, we use rajas to fuel effort with small steps that alleviate struggle."

(and other physiological reactions). But the downfall of being caught in the state of tamas is that it holds us back from entering into the process of creativity. Hence the need to calm and train the brain to catch those tumbling thoughts in the act! When we learn to root out unconscious or subconscious beliefs—misperceptions about what we "think" we are about to lose—and perhaps take action, life changes for the better.

"When we learn to root out unconscious or subconscious beliefs—misperceptions about what we "think" we are about to lose—and perhaps take action, life changes for the better."

Again, for the purpose of Westernizing, tamas will be renamed *Dord*. The word *dord* first appeared in an English dictionary around 1934. The word, however, never really (officially!) existed. The following describes the mishap: "Dord is a notable error in lexicography, an accidental creation of the G. and C. Merriam Company's staff included in the second edition of its New International Dictionary, in which the term is defined as density" (Dord, n.d.).

The word "dord" was never real. Similarly, many of our thoughts and perceptions about struggle, loss, and being stuck may seem real in the moment but, more often than not, arise from, and are deeply rooted in, the fear of loss. Thus, *Dord* is the perfect word to describe aspects of our lives that cause us to feel and act smaller than the powerful beings we really are.

The truth is that no one person is entirely Sazy, Rawk, or Dord. Rather, each of us is a combination of the three and the trick is to keep them in balance. We need Sazy for genuinely positive thoughts—not based on *conscious striving*. We need the action of Rawk to take small steps and risks towards an intention—not *frantic action*. We need to be aware of the deceptive nature of Dord playing tricks on the brain—and not be drawn into the abyss of *heaviness/inertia*. Once the Outer Triangle of Thuse is balanced, the brain begins to quiet. We become able to hear quiet guidance as we enter into the Inner Triangle.

12

THE OUTER TRIANGLE

dord, rawk, & sazy

Whatever your first thought might be, it's what you do after that initial thought that determines your ability to move forth with an endeavor.

CHAPTER TWELVE

TRIANGLE OF THUSE: THE OUTER TRIANGLE

You have been asked to consider quite a bit of information in the past eleven chapters. Parts of the narrative have included light-hearted, human-interest stories while other sections have offered scientific data combined with philosophical viewpoints. We've explored, dug, and traveled down multiple rabbit holes. Bravo!

To summarize, we've uncovered the hazards of stress and the negative effects of a reactive brain. That's why it's so important for the brain to stay calm by functioning from the cerebral cortex. We also know that addressing stress in a purposeful and direct way opens the door for the brainwaves to synchronize, not only insuring a calm brain but also making innovative ideas possible. Further, we've addressed how just one negative thought can start a tumble, an avalanche, of other adverse thoughts—ending in struggle and blocking us from experiencing the process of creativity. On the flip side, ongoing effort builds neural networks of learning and productive habits while paving the way for effortless effort, a process that leads us into effortlessness. Finally, we've taken on the big bad wolves of procrastination and unchecked perfectionism. That's a lot of information. But ... we're not quite done yet.

In later chapters, we moved away from aspects of the brain, attempting to understand the unquantifiable mind through the lens of string theory. We examined the phenomenon of vibration, exemplified by Emoto's water crystals and Chladni's sound images, and how our vibration can affect our daily lives. Finally, we explored three levels of effortlessness that allow us to thrive—facilitating our process of creativity, enhancing our ability

"We also know that addressing stress in a purposeful and direct way opens the door for the brainwaves to synchronize, not only insuring a calm brain but also making innovative ideas possible."

to manifest what fulfills desires, and allowing us to enter into the Mind of Thuse.

Throughout the book I've sprinkled real-life solutions that stress the importance of building your own tool kit of techniques, especially when dealing with the reactive brain. The purpose of each and every little piece of information is to assist you with the development of your process of creativity—leading to effort, effortless effort, effortlessness, and the Mind of Thuse. Now, it's time to expand how all this information intersects and interweaves. It's time to expand on the *visual* representation of the Triangle of Thuse.

Previously, we've established that the Triangle of Thuse contains an Outer and an Inner Triangle. The Outer Triangle represents three behavioral aspects: Sazy, Rawk, and Dord. As a visual referent, the Triangle underscores the importance of *balance*. When balanced, these behaviors form the stable structure of an Outer Triangle. The Outer Triangle then becomes the emotional and mental support required to activate enthusiasm, calmness, and focus—aspects found within the Inner Triangle (to be discussed in the next chapter).

Though the Triangle is stable when the behavioral aspects are balanced, if unbalanced then it can quickly collapse in on itself.

Though the Triangle is stable when the behavioral aspects are balanced, if unbalanced then it can quickly collapse in on itself. Think about sitting on a three-legged stool. If one leg is slightly shorter, you can still sit on that stool; however, it may be wobbly and uncomfortable. If one leg continues to shorten, you and the stool will soon topple to the ground—so, too, with the three legs of the Outer Triangle. And … the process all starts with a single thought.

WHAT TO DO WITH THAT FIRST THOUGHT?

Do you have a great idea that you want to bring forward? Perhaps you've been thinking about writing a novel, creating a new software app, or buying a co-op farm in Canada. Are you able to freely exclaim: "Wow! I really want to develop this idea!"? Will you be excited about the potential and proceed, or will your brain become reactive?

If an initial thought runs contrary to long-held beliefs and perceptions (for example, "I don't have enough time, energy,

"Wow! I really want to develop this idea!"

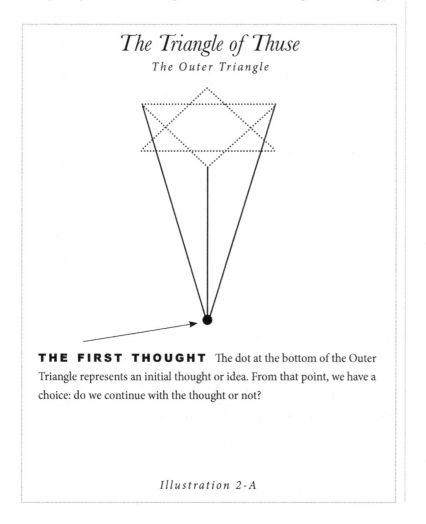

The Triangle of Thuse
The Outer Triangle

THE FIRST THOUGHT The dot at the bottom of the Outer Triangle represents an initial thought or idea. From that point, we have a choice: do we continue with the thought or not?

Illustration 2-A

or money!"), the brain will trigger a chain of reactive emotions. Your next thought is likely to be something along these lines: "I really want to take on writing a novel … but it will probably *never* happen." Subsequent thoughts and emotions may then run the gamut from "I hate my job!" to "I feel stuck and it makes me so angry!" Been there, done that, and it's not a pretty picture.

Whatever your first thought might be, it's what you do after that initial thought that determines the balance (or not) of the Triangle of Thuse. Now, let's look at the illustration of the Outer Triangle of Thuse and, more specifically, at the black dot located at the bottom of the Triangle. The dot represents the initial thought or idea. From that black dot, the thought or idea extends upward along the sides of the Outer Triangle. For the Triangle to assume a well-balanced form, you must keep Sazy, Rawk, and Dord in alignment, or balance.

Here's the clincher: if one side of the Triangle becomes challenged by any distracting thought(s) from the reactive brain, then the Outer Triangle may lean too far in one direction, causing a loss of balance. The stable structure could then crumble and fall. The good news is that we don't have to build a *perfect* Outer Triangle to enter the Inner Triangle—just as we can sit on that three-legged stool even if it is slightly off balance. However, continually building and strengthening our Outer Triangle is all important in order to gain entry into the Inner Triangle and thereby experience the realms of effortlessness.

When Sazy's happiness is based on internal well-being rather than any external circumstance, one leg of the stool—or, in this case, one side of the Triangle—will fully extend. When our

"Here's the clincher: if one side of the Triangle becomes challenged by any distracting thought(s) from the reactive brain, then the Outer Triangle may lean too far in one direction, causing a loss of balance."

happiness is based on internal well-being, the second leg or side (Rawk) is able to take small steps of action without becoming frantic. Finally, when we follow these two aspects with a quiet brain—a brain that has calmly resisted the trap of Dord—then the third side extends. The results? Through effort, the Outer Triangle builds structure and establishes a supportive base, like the three-legged stool, to enhance your process of creativity.

Through Sazy's positive outlook, and by taking small action steps with Rawk, we are able to monitor the brain's antics and avoid falling prey to Dord. I cannot emphasize this strongly enough: your laudable idea—represented by the dot at the bottom of the Outer Triangle—can easily be taken hostage by the brain's reactions. When this happens, there will be no extension of the other two sides to build your Triangle.

Now let's turn to a scenario that typifies this dynamic. A friend of mine, Greg, was trying to write and illustrate a children's book in his spare time. Focusing on this project, and with a full-time job, he was burning the candle at both ends. Yet Greg was able to handle the challenge easily because he experienced such fulfillment from the process of creativity. His Outer Triangle remained in balance, as his "juices" easily flowed more effortlessly than not. But one day he called me in distress.

He had a new boss at work. As a result, Greg's assigned tasks had doubled over the past three months. Although he liked his job, Greg was clearly suffering from fatigue and teetering on the edge of fight, flight, or freeze. Workplace frustrations had caused his beta brainwaves to be overly stimulated. Furthermore, Greg had drawn back from his own creative project and had not

"I cannot emphasize this strongly enough: your laudable idea—represented by the dot at the bottom of the Outer Triangle—can easily be taken hostage by the brain's reactions."

written or drawn anything for the past four weeks. What had happened?

Evidently, the structure of his Outer Triangle had become significantly unbalanced. As a result, it was impossible for Greg to enter into his process of creativity. So I inquired about his thought process. He confessed that he was struggling and angry regarding the changes at work. However, Greg agreed to put more effort into monitoring his thoughts and also started taking yoga again to affect his vibration. (Gentle reminder: how one affects vibration is a unique and personal choice.) He also agreed to repeat a simple question throughout the day: "What am I going to do with my next thought?" Within two weeks, Greg called to report that he was once again happily at work on his book. In addition, his tasks at work seemed to be less arduous and frustrating. The outcome was extremely positive due to Greg consciously putting in the time and effort to make it so.

How will you keep yourself balanced in the Outer Triangle so that you may enter into the Inner Triangle easily, with least effort? Regardless of the answer, what is hugely important is vigilance. What you are going to do with your next thought makes all the difference … and gives you moments of choice. Will you fall into the clutches of Dord or not?

FIRST SIDE OF THE OUTER TRIANGLE: DORD

The first leg side of the Outer Triangle is Dord, or "the moment of choice." By now we know that Dord loves to argue and convince us of the need to struggle. Dord is the reactive, hyperactive brain that creates a high frequency beta brainwave state. This

"What you are going to do with your next thought makes all the difference … and gives you moments of choice."

state causes unwanted chemicals to course throughout the body: chemicals related to stress; to the behaviors of fight, flight or freeze; and to the release of adrenaline. Dord represents procrastination, unchecked perfectionism, and lack of self-confidence. Dord causes us to believe that we cannot change and, as a result, prevents us from moving forward with a new endeavor. Dord's favorite statement is: "I can't because of x, y, or z." Dord only sees black and white when in fact other

"Dord represents procrastination, unchecked perfectionism, and lack of self-confidence."

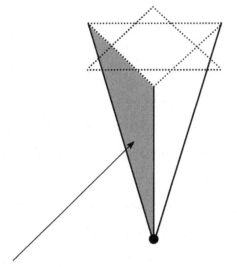

The Triangle of Thuse
The Outer Triangle

DORD Hello Dord! So your first thought has come and gone. What are you going to with your next thought? If resistance shows up, Dord may cause an avalanche of unwanted thoughts. In reaction, Dord may toggle the brain into flight, fight, or freeze and perhaps a high frequency beta brainwave state as you become unable to remain calm and focus on the task at hand. Dord creates struggle and insists, "I cannot!!" Well ... actually, you can. You are not your Dord.

Illustration 2-B

options may be available. Dord creates fear, keeping us stuck in the quicksand of distrust, doubt, and judgment towards self and others. Furthermore, lying hidden within Dord are negative conscious thoughts that, in combination with other subconscious and unconscious emotions and thought patterns, wreak havoc on our well-being.

The problem with Dord is that it cannot get out of its own way! It has no ability to soothe the nagging conscious thoughts or root out negative subconscious and unconscious thought processes. For example, in a moment's inspiration, you might say to yourself, "I'm going to quit my job, travel to Tuscany, take cooking lessons, and learn how to be a chef." The conscious portion of the brain is excited and in agreement with that thought. However, buried in the deep recesses of the subconscious and unconscious are old ingrained beliefs and perceptions that reply: only crazy people leave behind a comfortable job! Your unconscious and subconscious thoughts battle for dominance with your conscious thoughts. More than likely, the idea will be abandoned as Dord exerts full control.

A word to the wise: Dord is the result of automatic brain responses that originally protected us from roaming dinosaurs. Period. The brain wants us to feel safe (and does not want you to quit your job and move to Tuscany!). Dord's protective mechanism is problematic, however, when it holds us back from taking those risks that deeply enhance our life experience. How to override Dord? Glad you asked.

"The brain wants us to feel safe (and does not want you to quit your job and move to Tuscany!)."

SECOND SIDE OF THE TRIANGLE: SAZY

The second side of the Outer Triangle is Sazy—what I refer to as "learned optimism." Sazy is the result of a calm brain accompanying synchronized brainwaves. Sazy is hip to Dord and its many sneaky tricks. Sazy's watchful eye knows how to reason with Dord, especially when it's knocking at the door preparing us to fight, fly, or freeze. Sazy knows how to talk Dord off the ledge of struggle. How? By differentiating between an individual's pessimism and learned optimism.

Consider my friend Greg once again. If he had viewed those four long weeks of writer's block as all encompassing and permanent, then he would have been labeled a pessimist. Moreover, Greg might have fallen into the trap of Dord: "I can't write! I should give up on this project because I am much too busy at work." What do you imagine Greg would have done with his next thought? With struggle taking over front and center, not only would Greg's Outer Triangle have become unbalanced but also he would have built a neural network habituated to struggle. Not so good.

Instead, Greg held the following thoughts: "I've not been productive with my writing for the past few weeks. Perhaps I need a vacation. Even better, I might need to ask my boss to assign some of my work duties to someone else. Now, how can I calm down my brain and synchronize my brainwaves?" This type of response allows an individual to recognize, acknowledge, and productively respond to a pessimistic mind-set—not only

"Sazy is the result of a calm brain accompanying synchronized brainwaves. Sazy is hip to Dord and its many sneaky tricks."

in regard to her/himself but in relationship to others, as well (Seligman, 2007). Greg's scenario is a good example of learned optimism.

Learned optimism, which can be strengthened through daily practice, allows an individual to view the outcome of an event as a temporary setback rather than a permanent situation (Seligman, 2007). In this way, one finds opportunity—slowly shifting one's thoughts from that of struggle to that of effort

"When learned optimism is in the driver's seat, Sazy is in balance and is able to offset Dord."

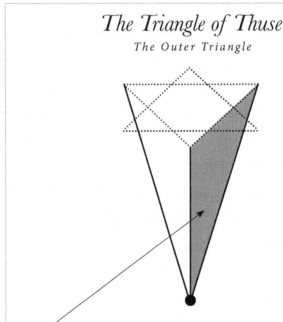

The Triangle of Thuse
The Outer Triangle

SAZY Sazy, the second side of the Outer Triangle, is well aware of the many antics of Dord. Sazy is always in the background ready to soothe Dord with learned optimism and positive statements that are combined with deep feeling. Sazy works with Rawk to halt the beginnings of unwanted thoughts while helping to build thoughts of contentment.

Illustration 2-C

146

combined with a more positive outlook. When learned optimism is in the driver's seat, Sazy is in balance and is able to offset Dord.

Let's take one final glance back at Greg's scenario. In practicing learned optimism, Greg thought it would be best to repeat a positive affirmation daily. He believed this affirmation would bring him real change. However, after a few months, Greg met me for a cup of coffee and confessed that the affirmation was not working. I asked him: are you repeating the affirmation in a way that sounds dry, rote, and repetitive? Or, are you infusing the affirmation with deep feelings of love, gratitude, and joy? Then I suggested that he juice up the affirmation with the deepest, most positive feelings he could muster. In this way, Sazy (rather than Dord) would be in control.

"Then I suggested that he juice up the affirmation with the deepest, most positive feelings he could muster. In this way, Sazy (rather than Dord) would be in control."

After our meeting, one more thought occurred to me: Greg most likely was being influenced by underlying unconscious and subconscious beliefs running counter to his affirmation. Uncovering those unconscious and subconscious Dord beliefs was the key to liberating his Sazy feelings and fueling the fire of affirmation. Greg, like the rest of us, deserved the feelings of learned optimism, joy, and happiness that Sazy brings, effectively offsetting the antics of Dord. What is another ally in offsetting Dord? None other than Rawk.

THIRD SIDE OF THE TRIANGLE: RAWK

Rawk, symbolizing "action," helps Sazy uncover unconscious or subconscious negative perceptions and behavioral patterns for which Dord is responsible. As part of the interplay of the Outer Triangle, Rawk represents effort in action ... without the need to struggle. The ongoing effort of Rawk helps individuals like Greg consistently take small steps when engaged in a large project. At its best, Rawk steadfastly takes small steps and allows for a small amount of risk-taking in the process of completing an endeavor.

Our Far Eastern friends in Japan understand the psychological benefit of making incremental, gradual changes. Japanese auto companies regularly practice a technique called Kaizen, meaning "improvement" or "change for the better."

"Rawk, symbolizing 'action,' helps Sazy uncover unconscious or subconscious negative perceptions and behavioral patterns for which Dord is responsible."

The Triangle of Thuse
The Outer Triangle

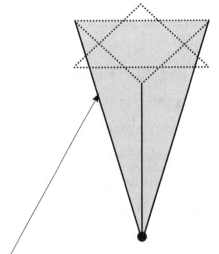

RAWK Rawk is the effort we put at the beginning of an endeavor. Working hand in hand with Sazy, Rawk takes incremental steps and risks while making small changes. In addition, Rawk and Sazy keep a watchful eye on Dord to maintain balance of the Outer Triangle. Note: Rawk is the back side of the Triangle.

Illustration 2-D

Kaizen is actually based on two Japanese words: "'Kai' meaning school and 'Zen' meaning wisdom" (Hudgik, n.d.). This philosophy encourages employees to implement a system of change or continuous improvement. Each company employee must make 60 to 70 suggestions per year regarding small improvements or changes. This practice allows for employees to remain calm, alter nonproductive habits, and participate creatively. Doesn't this sound like Rawk at its best?

However, Rawk at its worst falls for the tricks of Dord and plunges into angst and anxiety. This is what happens, for example, when we frantically rush to meet a deadline—or, despondent and hopeless, give up on our endeavor altogether.

Remember that Rawk facilitates one's ability to take large, seemingly overwhelming tasks and divide them into small manageable chunks. In this manner, the brain remains calm while the task is completed, step by step. Therefore, the job is done more effortlessly than not—without adrenaline rushes or procrastination!

Finally, Rawk and Sazy walk hand in hand—engaging in a delicate exchange—to help Dord remain quiet and tranquil, and thus in balance. While Sazy promotes deep feeling and positive activity, Rawk also plays a significant role in that it is effort—taking small steps and risks. Without Sazy, Rawk may be driven uncontrollably, and with intense stress, towards completing a task. Without Rawk, Sazy is unable to take action. Working in harmony, these two sides of the Outer Triangle competently check Dord's negative behaviors.

> *"Remember that Rawk facilitates one's ability to take large, seemingly overwhelming tasks and divide them into small manageable chunks."*

Although Dord is not an ally like Sazy and Rawk, it is important to befriend and develop compassion towards Dord. Remember, Dord is nothing more than automatic and reactionary responses from the brain. When we understand the true nature of Dord, and develop strategies for working with the dynamic interplay of these three aspects, the Outer Triangle becomes balanced—allowing us easy access to the attributes of the Inner Triangle!

13

possibilities & tendencies

Our Inner Triangle is full of these tendencies—intangible,
unformed thoughts or energy—simply waiting for manifestation,
waiting to be "birthed" by our actions arising from the
Outer Triangle.

CHAPTER THIRTEEN

THE INNER TRIANGLE OF THUSE

Saturday mornings at my home are sheer bliss. I get up, brew a cup of joe, plop into my command-central chair, and begin to write. This morning ritual has been ongoing and effortless for years. Yet something entirely unexpected happened when I launched into this chapter. Indeed, writing about the topic at hand—how effortlessness is experienced within the Inner Triangle of Thuse—found me anything but blissful. The book was only three weeks away from meeting printer deadlines for galleys (first proofs). Yet I still had not "put pen to paper" on any part of the chapter. Yikes! Although a portion of the chapter had been written a year earlier, it occurred to me—somewhere between sipping morning coffee and feeding the cats—that much, if not all, of what I had previously written no longer applied! A rewrite was definitely in order.

"... I was wise to the shenanigans of Dord! With Sazy and Rawk on my side, my Outer Triangle remained in balance and therefore I was able to easily problem solve."

As I began staring at the blank page on my computer, a distracting thought or two about that looming deadline tried to upset the balance of my Outer Triangle. However, I was wise to the shenanigans of Dord! With Sazy and Rawk on my side, my Outer Triangle remained in balance and therefore I was able to easily problem solve. Sazy helped me to remain positive while Rawk helped me to glean relevant information from my graduate papers. So ... I started digging.

An hour and a half later, after cutting and pasting from multiple papers, I was clearly heading in the wrong direction. Something was undeniably amiss. Finally, I "woke up" and realized my Outer Triangle had become seriously out of balance. Dord had snuck up on me once again.

The day before, a disturbing situation at work had left me feeling upset and stressed. Almost 24 hours later, adrenaline was still pumping through my system, and the pit of my stomach remained tight with anxiety. Even my trusty tool kit of calming techniques had fallen short in dissipating problematic chemicals generated by my reactive brain. As a result, I literally could not think clearly. And … the writing process was anything but effortless—in fact, quite the opposite.

So I took a break. I walked away from that blank computer screen and headed out the door to grab a couple of breakfast tacos. Driving my car happens to be a reliable calming tool. Countless ideas have presented themselves and complex problems have been solved while doing nothing more than waiting at a traffic light. The act of driving allows my brainwaves to slow down and perhaps even synchronize. Within a few minutes of backing out of the driveway, the introduction for this chapter had become evident and … I had had a really good chuckle. Furthermore, all of you had been saved from having to read dry research pulled from a not-so-interesting graduate paper!

Two savory tacos and several deep breaths later, I was back at the computer. Although still not *entirely* calm, I noticed the words beginning to pour from my fingertips more effortlessly than not. To continue calming my brain, I plugged in earbuds and listened to an old standby: "Into the Creative State." This soothing music—that I wrote specifically to ease the brain into an alpha brainwave state—*always* supports my process of creativity.

"Even my trusty tool kit of calming techniques had fallen short in dissipating problematic chemicals generated by my reactive brain."

The results? With the efforts of Rawk and the encouragement of Sazy, my Outer Triangle began to rebalance. Although my Outer Triangle was not *totally* in balance, just the act of starting to write helped me focus and calm myself even more. As new sentences poured onto the page, the energy of enthusiasm took hold. There was no doubt: Thuse had begun to surface once more!

Soon I slipped into an alpha/theta brainwave state, as my breathing became deep and even. What felt like 15 minutes turned out to be, in actuality, two hours of nonstop writing. Time had become suspended while I effortlessly flowed within my Inner Triangle. At this point you might be asking: what oh what is in that Inner Triangle that is so extraordinary? Very glad you asked.

"Although my Outer Triangle was not totally in balance, just the act of starting to write helped me focus and calm myself even more."

THE OUTER TRIANGLE: FINAL THOUGHTS

Before we explore the Inner Triangle, let's do a quick recap of the Outer Triangle. Remember that the Outer Triangle structure consists of three sides—Dord, Sazy, and Rawk. Think of these sides as the physical framework or structure that holds together an idea or endeavor. For instance, a painter must have a canvas—and paint to cover that canvas—in order to produce a painting that will communicate her/his newest idea. The canvas and paint allow for the physical manifestation of the idea.

Just as the canvas and paint provide a framework for the artist's ideas, so, too, does the Outer Triangle provide supportive framework for our ideas and creative endeavors. We are like the artist in that we also need the action and stability of Rawk and

Sazy, along with a quiet Dord, or our ideas will remain dormant in an unmanifested state. A balanced Outer Triangle supports our mental and emotional well-being while serving as a container through which ideas manifest from the vacuum of nothingness found in the Inner Triangle.

INSIDE THE INNER TRIANGLE

"Our Inner Triangle is full of these tendencies—intangible, unformed thoughts or energy—simply waiting manifestation, waiting to be 'birthed' by our actions arising from the Outer Triangle."

At last: the inner space of the Triangle. No canvas. No paints. Only concepts and ideas waiting to take shape out of the vacuum of nothingness. When the Outer Triangle is balanced, the Inner Triangle is full of invisible potential waiting to make itself known. Our Inner Triangle is full of these tendencies—intangible, unformed thoughts or energy—simply waiting for manifestation, waiting to be "birthed" by our actions arising from the Outer Triangle. It is my opinion that manifestation happens, much like Emoto's water crystals and Chladni's sound images, when we are resonating at the same vibrational frequency as our intent. Let me underscore this concept: Dr. Bruce Lipton states in his book, *Biology of Belief*, "We stick to the physical world of Newton and ignore the invisible quantum world of Einstein, in which matter is actually made up of energy and there are no absolutes. At the atomic level, matter does not exist with certainty; it only exists as a tendency to exist" (Lipton, 2008). In short, ideas such as those that wind up on a canvas are tendencies of energy that need the framework of the Outer Triangle to become manifest.

Now that we have familiarized ourselves with the tendencies of the Inner Triangle, how in the world do we get into it? Let's return to that little black dot at the bottom of the

Triangle. That dot represents an initial thought about a potential endeavor. Not only does the dot represent an initial thought but also one's corresponding enthusiasm for that endeavor. This enthusiasm is requisite for entering into the Inner Triangle.

Once inside the Triangle you may experience (either consciously, subconsciously, or unconsciously) seven steps: 1) enthusiasm, 2) calm brain, 3) focus, 4) inner listening to Thuse, 5) idea flow or problem solving, 6) response to the inner listening of Thuse, and 7) effortlessness, timelessness, and endless energy. While this seems like a step-by-step or paint-by-numbers approach, it is more of a guide to ascertain where you are within the fluidity of your own Inner Triangle. As such, these are not necessarily sequential steps, but rather interchangeable fluid movements that are not dependent upon time.

While it is necessary to experience the initial step of enthusiasm, steps two and three of a calm brain and focus are interchangeable. We all agree that a calm brain enhances our ability to focus, but it also works vice versa: the act of focusing can also calm the brain. However, the next three steps—four, five, and six: inner listening to Thuse, the idea or problem solving state, and response to Thuse—only occur sequentially and sometimes in such a quick succession that they seem to occur almost simultaneously. A good example of this? A calm and focused writer "hears" her/his inner Thuse and then quickly writes the sentence. For the writer, this "hearing" seems to be like receiving words from nowhere and the act of writing is the response. The hearing and writing can be almost simultaneous. The last state of "effortlessness, timelessness, and endless energy"

"Once inside the Triangle you may experience (either consciously, subconsciously, or unconsciously) seven steps: 1) enthusiasm, 2) calm brain, 3) focus, 4) inner listening to Thuse, 5) idea flow or problem solving, 6) response to the inner listening of Thuse, and 7) effortlessness, timelessness, and endless energy."

occurs after the writer has been consistently "hearing" and responding to Thuse over a period of time.

On another level, listening and responding to Thuse is not just task oriented, but can also extend into our daily lives— whether we are aware of it or not. I think of this level as the "call" of Thuse. Let me give you an example of an *unconscious* "call" of Thuse.

"The combination of George's ongoing focus with his strong, steadfast intention of obtaining a signature created an energetic vibration."

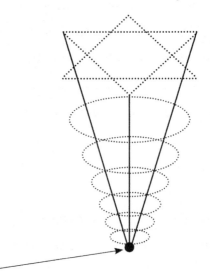

The Triangle of Thuse
The Inner Triangle

ENTHUSIASM As we continually feed enthusiasm, it fuels the energy of Thuse that, in turn, boosts effort to become more effortless than not. Enthusiasm carries us through times when we begin to doubt the validity of our endeavors. However, because enthusiasm can wane, and suddenly disappear in the blink of an eye, we must nurture it.

Illustration 3-A

George, a real estate agent, is holding the intention to obtain a final signature for a contract but has been unable to get in touch with the potential buyer. One afternoon, during an errand, he is suddenly and inexplicably pulled towards a certain grocery store. George may not fully understand this energetic pull to the grocery store but regardless he stops the car and gets out. Somewhere between the tomatoes and celery he spots the very person who needs and wants to sign the contract. George neatly arranges a meeting time and date to sign the contract. How did this happen?

The combination of George's ongoing focus with his strong, steadfast intention of obtaining a signature created an energetic vibration. This vibration resonated with the signee shopping at the grocery store and thus resulted in George being magnetically pulled into that environment. George was unaware of this subtle yet powerful, inner call of Thuse. He may have well considered the event as a synchronicity.

However, one can make a *conscious* choice to integrate Thuse into daily life by intentionally listening for the call of Thuse while focusing on a specific intention. Further, had George been conscious of the call, it would have been up to him to trust and respond to it accordingly. Being conscious of the call of Thuse can enhance the possibilities and tendencies of synchronicity.

"Being conscious of the call of Thuse can enhance the possibilities and tendencies of synchronicity."

ENTHUSIASM: WHAT'S THE APPEAL?

Think back to a favorite teacher, colleague, or friend for whom you developed deep respect. What strongly appealed to you about that person? Perhaps they were particularly inspirational or effervescent; the way they walked, talked, or interacted with others made a favorable impression on you. What has always attracted *me* about certain people is their sincerity and enthusiasm.

In chapter eleven, we discussed enthusiasm in depth. We know that enthusiasm translates to feeling calm yet excited, sure of ourselves, and open to possibilities and tendencies. As we continually feed enthusiasm, it fuels the energy of Thuse that, in turn, boosts effort to become more effortless than not. Enthusiasm carries us through times when we begin to doubt the validity of our endeavors. However, because enthusiasm can wane, and suddenly disappear in the blink of an eye, we must nurture it.

"As we continually feed enthusiasm, it fuels the energy of Thuse that, in turn, boosts effort to become more effortless than not. Enthusiasm carries us through times when we begin to doubt the validity of our endeavors."

Nurturing enthusiasm for a new endeavor is like caretaking a newborn infant—it needs to be attended to, fed, and protected. Why? Because lack of enthusiasm causes countless ideas with great potential to be dismissed and lost forever— considered fantasy, impossible, or just plain stupid. Whenever enthusiasm gets tossed out the window, the possibilities and tendencies rarely manifest. What if history's great inventors, artists, and entrepreneurs had dismissed their ideas when enthusiasm waned?

Dord does its best to squelch enthusiasm and harangues us with messages like "You're no Einstein!" For enthusiasm to be nurtured within the Inner Triangle, it is imperative to build that strong foundation of a balanced Outer Triangle. With Rawk and Sazy keeping a watchful eye on Dord, enthusiasm is able to generate the right amount of energy in the Inner Triangle—

propelling us forward to the next two steps: focus and a calm brain.

CALM BRAIN & FOCUS: QUIET & CLARITY

With increased enthusiasm comes the energy of Thuse and, with that, a natural urge to work on your project or endeavor. Interestingly enough, in tandem with the boost of energy generated by enthusiasm, we seem to also mysteriously find ample time and opportunity to work on that project. But often that energy and urge is not enough because we also need to be calm and focused. The solution for when we are too stressed, scattered, or distracted? Slow down the brainwave frequencies.

Let me clarify the importance of focus. Without focus, there is no "tipping the scale" from effort to effortless effort. Every writer knows what it's like to sit in front of a blank computer screen and feel uninspired. For instance, you may be at the computer trying to write the first chapter of a children's book yet accomplishing nothing more than staring at an empty page. Daunting? Discouraging? You bet, especially if you are stressed. But if you can begin to make a small effort to generate *something*, then focus can often follow. These small, completed tasks facilitate the release of stress by allowing one to relax into the slower alpha/theta brainwaves. For example, write a paragraph, solve a math problem, or pull out the tools of your trade. While the techniques for calming and focusing are endless, below are a few examples that serve me well.

When my beta brainwave frequency is too high, I plug in earbuds and listen to music specifically written to calm the brain.

"Without focus, there is no 'tipping the scale' from effort to effortless effort."

Another technique is to tell myself: just work on the project for five minutes and, after five minutes, you can simply walk away! But then I also promise myself to return to work on the project in another five minutes. This exercise of five minutes on and five minutes off generally calms my brain and assists with focus. Within a relatively short time, I am able to slip into an effortless state.

"There are great benefits from learning how to quiet the brain on cue. You're calm. You're focused. You're in the Inner Triangle and you begin to hear your inner Thuse."

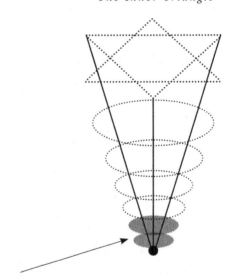

The Triangle of Thuse
The Inner Triangle

CALM BRAIN AND FOCUS Without a calm brain and focus there is no "tipping the scale" from effort to effortless effort. If you can begin to make a small effort to generate *something*, then focus will often follow. These small, completed tasks facilitate the release of stress by allowing one to relax into the slower alpha/theta brainwaves.

Illustration 3-B

Another favorite calming technique is deep, deep breathing from the belly up to the chest—with eyes closed while focusing on one point on the body. However, as I've previously noted, the number of calming techniques is endless. Find your favorites and utilize them when beginning any new endeavor. There are great benefits from learning how to quiet the brain on cue. You're calm. You're focused. You're in the Inner Triangle and you begin to hear your inner Thuse.

THE ASPECTS OF THE INNER TRIANGLE MEET THE ART OF THOUGHT

As stated above, within the Inner Triangle are potential concepts and ideas simply waiting to take form. To manifest such concepts and ideas, three invaluable aspects within the Inner Triangle must occur in sequence: 1) inner listening to Thuse, 2) problem solving or idea flow, and 3) a conscious response to Thuse. Even though these aspects must be sequential, oftentimes they occur almost simultaneously. To explore how these three aspects interact, and to understand how concepts and ideas are brought forth within the Inner Triangle, let's zero in on some relevant research.

You will recall that when an individual is stressed, frightened, or threatened, the reticular activating system (RAS) toggles thinking away from the creative, calm learning brain (the cerebral cortex) to the "fight or flight" of the limbic system (Howard, 1999, p. 47). This switching not only prevents the flow of ideas, or problem solving, but also causes an individual to experience the need for fight, fly, or freeze. Likewise, when the individual is calm, the toggle "switches the cortex back

"You will recall that when an individual is stressed, frightened, or threatened, the reticular activating system (RAS) toggles thinking away from the creative, calm learning brain (the cerebral cortex) to the 'fight or flight' of the limbic system."

on and allows creativity and logic to return to center stage"
(Howard, 1999, p. 47). These findings underscore the irrefutable
importance of a balanced Outer Triangle!

As for problem solving and ideation, multiple theories
currently abound. Some of the most relevant research comes
from theorist Graham Wallas, a pioneer in the area of creativity

*"... within the Inner Triangle
are potential concepts and
ideas simply waiting to
take form"*

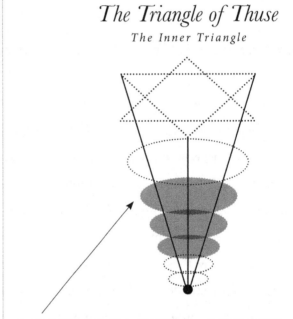

The Triangle of Thuse
The Inner Triangle

**LISTENING TO THUSE, PROBLEM
SOLVING AND IDEA FLOW, AND
CONSCIOUS RESPONSE TO THUSE** These three
aspects within the Inner Triangle are integral for the ideation and eureka
state. However, always remember that they must be fully supported not
only by a balanced Outer Triangle but also by subsequent enthusiasm,
focus, and a calm brain within the Inner Triangle.

Illustration 3-C

and author of *The Art of Thought*. For our purposes Wallas's theory on problem solving and idea flow serves to provide a certain amount of perspective and context on how the Triangle of Thuse handles problem solving and idea flow.

In 1926, Wallas categorized problem solving into five discrete phases: 1) preparation, 2) incubation, 3) intimation, 4) illumination, and 5) verification (Wallas, 1926). He further stated that if one is able to solve a problem quickly and easily, steps two through four are skipped. However, when stumped for a solution, the five phases remain sequential. Even though we are addressing the three invaluable aspects (introduced on page 163) of the Inner Triangle, we will also weave in some aspects of the Outer Triangle to compare Wallas's theory to the Triangle of Thuse.

"To further explore how Wallas's concept of preparation relates to the Triangle of Thuse, let's ask a relevant question: do you have the necessary skills to attempt your endeavor?"

THE ART OF THOUGHT: PREPARATION

The *preparation* phase is the accumulation of knowledge and deliberate preparatory work needed to focus on the problem to be solved (Wallas, 1926). For our purposes, the preparation phase most closely relates to the action of Rawk found in the Outer Triangle. To further explore how Wallas's concept of preparation relates to the Triangle of Thuse, let's ask a relevant question: do you have the necessary skills to attempt your endeavor?

Not long ago a dear friend had an idea about starting a business. She and her potential business partner came to my home for dinner one evening with the express purpose of discussing their direction. After a lengthy conversation, they decided on designing a clothing line. Here are the four questions I asked, accompanied by their responses: 1) Are you enthusiastic about this business venture? Both answered with a resounding "yes." 2) Do you know how to design and sew clothing? Both looked at each other and responded with a lukewarm "no." 3) Since you don't have the skills at present, do you know someone who can teach you? Both were unsure. 4) Are you willing to put in the necessary effort to learn the craft? Both answered, "No." At this point, I voiced concern that neither one was willing to put in requisite preparation for starting their new endeavor. Long story short, that new business never got off the ground.

If these potential partners had been willing to make the effort (Rawk) to accumulate knowledge (find someone to teach them the craft) and also put in the deliberate preparatory work (exert effort to learn the craft), they might be the proud owners of a clothing line today.

"Wallas's incubation phase closely relates to the aspect of Rawk associated with the Outer Triangle. Rawk helps us to step away from a project that is proving problematic and then later return to it. Yet, incubation is also related to the Inner Triangle because it resides on the fringes of inner listening to Thuse."

THE ART OF THOUGHT: INCUBATION

In Wallas's next problem-solving phase, *incubation*, we shift our thinking away from the problem at hand and instead work with the unconscious and involuntary mental aspects of our brain (Wallas, 1926). In this phase, the "deliberate, conscious problem-solving activity is suspended" (Dorfman, Kihlstrom, Shames, 1994). In other words, from a cognitive perspective, we stop trying to "figure out" how to solve the problem. Most likely, we are all familiar with this particular experience. For example, when we are "stumped" by a problem, we either give up or move away from it for a while.

Wallas's incubation phase closely relates to the aspect of Rawk associated with the Outer Triangle. Rawk helps us to step away from a project that is proving problematic and then later return to it. Yet, incubation is also related to the Inner Triangle because it resides on the fringes of inner listening to Thuse. When deliberate problem solving is suspended, surrendering to hearing an inner Thuse becomes possible—as we move closer to bringing forth the potential concepts and ideas that reside in the Inner Triangle.

For instance, when we take a break from the computer, that break time may be instrumental in percolating a solution. While doing laundry or washing dishes or even while listening to a lovely piece of music, we may not be consciously focusing on the problem. However, within the recesses of the brain these unsolved problems are actually incubating on the fringes of consciousness. Our inner Thuse can almost hear a solution.

Although incubation is sometimes the antithesis of a results-driven educational system (and society), it is nevertheless an essential requirement for the creative act (Raelin, 2002). Even though it does not seem we are doing much of anything during the incubation phase, the brain is, in fact, actively attempting to solve the problem. As we draw near to a solution, to hearing the inner Thuse, the next phase shows up: intimation.

"Although incubation is sometimes the antithesis of a results-driven educational system (and society), it is nevertheless an essential requirement for the creative act."

THE ART OF THOUGHT: INTIMATION

Some theorists treat Wallas's third phase, *intimation*, as a subset of illumination rather than its own distinct phase. Specifically, intimation refers to a feeling or knowing that an individual perceives when a solution is forthcoming. Wallas surmised that the rising and falling of consciousness is an indicator that the thinker knows a solution is forthcoming—in spite of not knowing the answer (Wallas, 1926). The intimation phase closely relates to the aspect of inner listening to Thuse found within the Inner Triangle, particularly when an individual has a feeling or knowing that "something" is about to happen.

Wallas describes intimation as "that moment in the illumination stage when our fringe-consciousness of an association-train is in the state of rising consciousness which indicates that the fully conscious flash of success is coming" (Wallas, 1926, p. 97). Later theorists have referred to this occurrence as *intuition* (Bowers, Farvolden, & Mermigis, 1995). According to Kenneth Bowers, whose primary area of research is intuition, it is a person's feeling "that a decision, judgment, or solution is correct, in the absence of supporting evidence, or even in the face of evidence to the contrary" (Bowers, 1994, pp. 613-617). But the term "intuition" does not always sit well with cognitive psychologists or, for that matter, with the scientific community. Even the general public tends to eschew its use. Whatever you call it—intimation or intuition—the notion is soft, fuzzy, and non-definable. Due to their subjective nature, intimation and intuition are difficult to pin down. Likewise, the inner listening of Thuse is of an unquantifiable nature.

For the most part, we all understand and have probably experienced the preparation and incubation phases when attempting to solve a problem. These phases seem more concrete in that they are described as deliberate. You may recall how scientists can readily research the physical brain but are faced with far more difficult challenges when researching and/or

"The intimation phase closely relates to the aspect of inner listening to Thuse found within the Inner Triangle, particularly when an individual has a feeling or knowing that 'something' is about to happen."

explaining the workings of the mind. As regards the research of intimation and intuition, a similar dilemma exists.

Yet, although exact definitions of intimation and intuition elude us, they are both very much a part of problem solving and idea flow within the Inner Triangle. Regardless of the name, the concept is this: we experience an unexplainable feeling of knowingness that communicates we're on the right track while solving a problem. Researchers theorize that this knowingness is based on previous learning—sort of like a name that you can't recall but is right on the tip of your tongue (Dorfman, Kihlstrom, Shames, 1994). However, inside the Inner Triangle, I propose that listening and responding to Thuse while problem solving and in idea flow is based not only on memory but also on a different kind of knowingness.

In an earlier chapter, we discussed the quantum world and string theory. Time to go a little deeper. In his book *The Cosmic Code,* the late Rockefeller University physicist Heinz Pagels suggests that quantum physics is like a code that interconnects everything together within the universe (Pagels, 1982). In addition, the theory of quantum entanglement deserves consideration. Described by Einstein as "spooky action at a distance," this theory states that particles of energy/matter are "entangled" in that they can communicate with each other instantaneously—regardless of the distance (Browne, 1997). In a twin-photon experiment by Dr. Nicolas Gisin of the University of Geneva, in the absence of any signal being transmitted between two photons, one of the photons "knew" what had just occurred to its twin. However, the twin was seven miles away! Further,

"... we experience an unexplainable feeling of knowingness that communicates we're on the right track while solving a problem."

the twin mimicked the transference of information at a speed of 186,282 miles per second (Browne, 1997). I cannot help but wonder if there is some part of us, beyond space and time, which just "knows" what it knows. But presently we have no idea how this knowingness knows! I propose that Thuse and the Mind of Thuse are those parts of ourselves that correlate to the twin photons in the experiments.

"While this phase of problem solving—call it intimation or intuition or Thuse— cannot be proven, seen, or measured, a world of inexplicable knowingness exists nevertheless."

I recently redecorated my home and experienced a simple example of this type of knowingness. My problem to solve was the following: I needed a large painting for my living room wall. But … I am super picky about the art that hangs in my home. A few days later, I stumbled upon a fund-raising event raffling off a lovely large painting. This painting was the exact size, color, and style that appealed to me. So … I purchased a five-dollar ticket.

Two weeks later, I found myself again in the area of the fund-raising event and overheard the business owner say he was going to pick the winner at 5:00 p.m. Within seconds, my inner Thuse whispered, "Buy three more tickets. You are going to win." So I did. I listened to Thuse and responded by buying more tickets. Furthermore, I knew without a doubt that the painting belonged on my wall. I just waited for the call at 5:00 p.m. My phone rang and the painting still hangs in my living room to this day.

While this phase of problem solving—call it intimation or intuition or Thuse—cannot be proven, seen, or measured, a world of inexplicable knowingness exists nevertheless. When this knowingness works in tandem with the preconscious processing of intimation, we are able to bring forth the latent concepts and ideas residing within the Inner Triangle. Now let's move forward to the next phase: illumination.

THE ART OF THOUGHT: ILLUMINATION

When enough information is gathered to solve a problem (preparation or Rawk) and we are able to listen and respond to Thuse (intimation and incubation) the next phase, *illumination,* is primed. Illumination is the moment when a new idea appears in the brain of the thinker; that is, "where the creative idea bursts forth from its preconscious processing into conscious awareness" (Wallas, 1926). Illumination is the effect of incubation and intimation. According to researchers, as the brain becomes tranquil, eureka moments—or the phase of illumination— activate in "the superior temporal sulcus that signifies the awareness of a new idea" (Carter, 2009, p. 168). Illumination is that eureka moment; it's the Aha! thought. It's what Einstein experienced. But it's also what we all experience in our daily lives—especially when we understand and utilize the process of creativity. Illumination is akin to the Inner Triangle aspects of idea flow and problem solving ... and conscious response to Thuse.

"Illumination is akin to the Inner Triangle aspects of idea flow and problem solving ... and conscious response to Thuse."

Prior to the phase of illumination, problem solving and ideation depend on information transfer between the hemispheres of the brain. For example, the right hemisphere— seat of creative abilities and visual awareness—is, more than likely, where the incubation phase or contemplation occurs (Bogen, 2000, pp. 341-369). Particularly important in the ideation phase is the corpus callosum, which transfers information from the right hemisphere of "visual awareness, creative abilities, and spatial-temporal awareness" to the left hemisphere of "reasoning and analysis" (Carter, 2009, p. 57). The evolution and harvest of creative output depends on the relaying of this information between the hemispheres (Moore et al., 2009). According to research, this point of transference between the two hemispheres has the highest potential for the ideation state to occur.

"The three aspects within the Inner Triangle—listening to Thuse, problem solving and idea flow, and a conscious response to Thuse—are integral for the ideation and eureka state."

Nikola Tesla, a Serbian-American inventor, engineer, and physicist, was best known for his contributions to the development of alternating current electrical supply. However, a particular solution eluded him for years. Then one day while taking a leisurely walk and, it is said, while quoting Faust, the solution suddenly came to him in a eureka moment. Tesla grabbed a stick and drew a diagram in the dirt to demonstrate how alternating current would work. The solution had needed to incubate for many years before illuminating as a solution, one that may have been based on previous learning or perhaps a level of knowingness (Sci, 2012). For our purposes, within the Inner Triangle of Thuse, when problem solving becomes second nature, then idea flow is ongoing as eureka moments easily arise. That's a pretty big statement. But it's true.

THE ART OF THOUGHT: VERIFICATION

Verification requires that we test and refine our ideas. The solution may need tweaking. If tweaking the solution to the problem does not produce satisfactory results, we need to go through Wallas's phases once again. How many times have we considered an idea to be brilliant only to apply it and realize that it still needs a lot of work?

The three aspects within the Inner Triangle—listening to Thuse, problem solving and idea flow, and a conscious response to Thuse—are integral for the ideation and eureka state. However, always remember that these three aspects must be fully supported not only by a balanced Outer Triangle but also by subsequent enthusiasm, focus, and a calm brain within the Inner Triangle.

Moreover, the five phases of problem solving suggested by Wallas provide context for the different aspects of the Triangle of Thuse. For instance, the effort of Rawk compares to Wallas's preparation phase. Rawk's ability to walk away from a project (temporarily) is also similar to the incubation phase. The intimation and illumination phases are comparable to the three aspects of the Inner Triangle: listening to Thuse, problem solving and idea flow, and a conscious response to Thuse. Now we get to wrap up the Inner Triangle with one more aspect—effortlessness, timelessness, and endless energy.

"How many times have we considered an idea to be brilliant only to apply it and realize that it still needs a lot of work?!"

EFFORTLESSNESS, TIMELESSNESS, AND ENDLESS ENERGY

I want to end this chapter with a story about Tom, a well-trained artist. Tom has become amazingly familiar with, and adept at, using the Triangle of Thuse. In a matter of seconds, he is able to focus intently and begin painting. As Tom continues to paint, his brain quiets on cue. Without forethought, and as stillness and focus increase, Tom dips his brush into a color and strokes it onto the canvas effortlessly.

The time in which Tom's listening to Thuse, problem solving, and responding to Thuse occurs instantaneously. With the Outer Triangle balanced and his ability to reside deeply within the Inner Triangle, Tom effortlessly listens to Thuse as the next paint stroke and the next appear on his canvas. One hour of painting turns into two as his focus continues to quiet his brain. The passing hours give rise to effortlessness, timelessness, and

"... within the Inner Triangle of Thuse, when problem solving becomes second nature, then idea flow is ongoing as eureka moments easily arise."

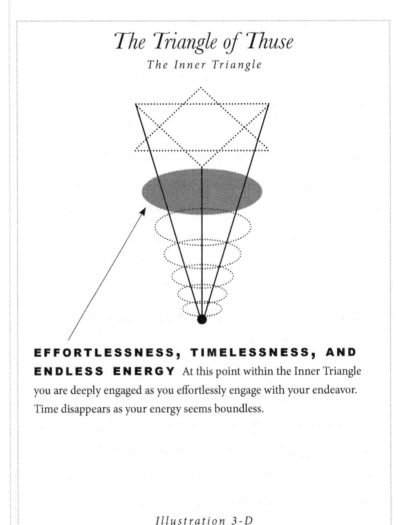

The Triangle of Thuse
The Inner Triangle

EFFORTLESSNESS, TIMELESSNESS, AND ENDLESS ENERGY At this point within the Inner Triangle you are deeply engaged as you effortlessly engage with your endeavor. Time disappears as your energy seems boundless.

Illustration 3-D

boundless energy. Tom becomes the painter allowing the painting to paint itself.

As Tom taps into this level of effortlessness, his thinking brain begins to surrender into nonthinking, as he aligns with the underlying fabric of the universe through the Mind of Thuse. Moment by moment, Tom is now operating in a powerful void of knowingness, beyond intuition. He is trusting his next action without a thought of what that next action might be. As Tom will

"... a powerful aspect of the Triangle of Thuse is this ability to ease away from the thinking brain and flow into the effortless nonthinking knowingness that is the Mind of Thuse."

The Triangle of Thuse
The Inner Triangle

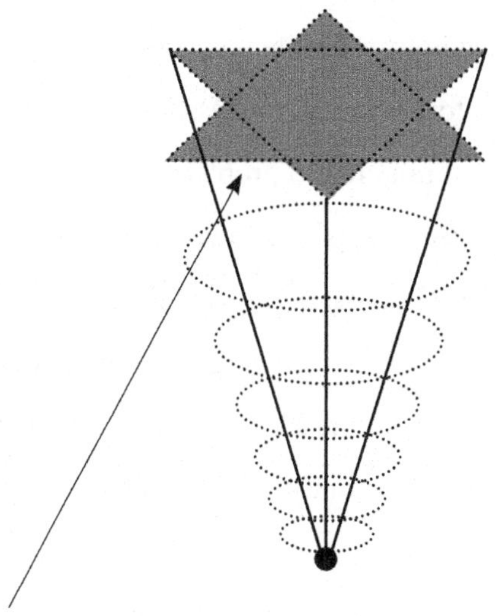

THE MIND OF THUSE The thinking brain begins to surrender into nonthinking, as one aligns with the underlying fabric of the universe through the Mind of Thuse. Moment by moment, you begin to operate in a powerful void of knowingness without a thought of what the next action might be.

Illustration 3-E

tell you: *a powerful aspect of the Triangle of Thuse is this ability to ease away from the thinking brain and flow into the effortless nonthinking knowingness that is the Mind of Thuse.* I know—a really big leap. But there it is.

BRING IT ON HOME

In summary, the Inner Triangle of Thuse is full of *tendencies*—intangible, unformed thoughts or energy—simply waiting to be "birthed" by our actions arising from the Outer Triangle and by enthusiasm for the project or endeavor. All aspects of the Inner Triangle—enthusiasm leading to Thuse, calm brain, focus, listening to Thuse, idea flow or problem solving, responding to Thuse, and finally effortlessness, timelessness, and endless energy—may be applied not only to problem solving the task at hand but also to multiple areas within your life. The Inner Triangle aspects of effortlessness, timelessness, and endless energy, while supporting problem solving and idea flow, reliably pave the way for experiencing the Mind of Thuse—that exquisite ability to slip into a powerful nonthinking mind.

"The Inner Triangle aspects of effortlessness, timelessness, and endless energy, while supporting problem solving and idea flow, reliably pave the way for experiencing the Mind of Thuse—that exquisite ability to slip into a powerful nonthinking mind."

14

a dynamic system

Even while you may not produce the work of Monet, you do have

the ability to vibrate with enthusiasm and contentment derived

from your own inner Thuse.

CHAPTER FOURTEEN

A DYNAMIC SYSTEM

Now that we have discussed the structure of the Triangle of Thuse, let's explore its relationship to the process of creativity and to the Mind of Thuse. The Triangle of Thuse is a dynamic system, intricately weaving the process of creativity with behavioral aspects of the Outer Triangle and possibilities and tendencies of the Inner Triangle. As we have discovered, the Outer Triangle includes multiple activities such as learning optimism, taking small steps, and risk taking which is part of the effort of preparation. Other aspects only found in the Inner Triangle such as enthusiasm, a calm brain, focus, and listening and responding to Thuse are the domain of effortless effort and effortlessness. It is important to realize that the aspects of both the Outer and the Inner Triangle must work in tandem with one another for one to successfully engage within the process of creativity. It is by mastering the dynamic, interweaving nature of the Outer and Inner Triangles that we not only enhance our process of creativity but also connect to, and thrive within, the Mind of Thuse. Yet, like mastering any craft or task, this process takes awareness and practice.

To summarize the Triangle's dynamic nature, let's take a closer step-by-step look at how the process of creativity works in tandem with the Outer and Inner Triangles.

"It is by mastering the dynamic, interweaving nature of the Outer and Inner Triangles that we not only enhance our process of creativity but also connect to, and thrive within, the Mind of Thuse."

STEP ONE

• Balance the Outer Triangle by calming the reactive brain (we're talking beta brainwaves!).

- Cultivate learned optimism and keep a watchful eye on Dord.
- Take small steps or risks within the process of creativity and give yourself permission to walk away (temporarily) from a project (preparation and incubation).

STEP TWO

"... when trying to balance your Outer Triangle, it's not unusual to find yourself seesawing between struggle and effort."

With the Outer Triangle balanced and a flow of enthusiasm we move into the Inner Triangle of possibilities and tendencies.

STEP THREE

- Once inside the Inner Triangle, allow your enthusiasm to transform into the energy of Thuse.
- Notice that the process of creativity has enabled your task at hand to become more effortless than not.

STEP FOUR

- Continue to calm, focus, and listen to your inner Thuse (intimation) as you move further into the Inner Triangle.
- Notice that problem solving, idea flow, and illumination are enhanced.
- Responding to your inner Thuse, slip into effortlessness, timelessness, and endless energy. Enjoy the process of creativity!

FINAL STEP

When your effortlessness accompanies the nonthinking state, notice that you are connected to the Mind of Thuse.

Understanding how all the different components of the Triangle of Thuse dynamically interweave is one thing. Getting the process started (i.e., forming the Triangle) is quite another. As with all new ventures (and adventures!), we get to start exactly where we are. Remember: in the initial stages of a new endeavor, we may not have the appropriate skill levels to pursue the task at hand. As a result, we may have to exert initial effort to acquire these skills. Also, as a reminder: when trying to balance your Outer Triangle, it's not unusual to find yourself seesawing between struggle and effort. However, once the Outer Triangle is balanced, *all seven steps of the Inner Triangle can take place within minutes*, as you move from effortless effort to effortlessness and, ultimately, to the Mind of Thuse. Yes, the process of quickly balancing the Outer Triangle, flowing through the steps of the Inner Triangle and easily connecting to the Mind of Thuse requires practice. The good news is that, with practice, the entire process will eventually feel like second nature.

"However, once the Outer Triangle is balanced, all seven steps of the Inner Triangle can take place within minutes, as you move from effortless effort to effortlessness and, ultimately, to the Mind of Thuse."

DEANNA LEARNS TO CODE

Underlying the concept of the Triangle of Thuse is the ability to distinguish struggle and effort, effortless effort, and effortlessness. These are all very different experiences. Struggle can predictably cause our Outer Triangle to collapse, making it impossible to enter into the Inner Triangle. However, with awareness and effort—and as one learns to take small steps accompanied by enthusiasm—eventually obstacles into the Inner Triangle will be surmounted. Keep in mind there is always a dynamic play between maintaining a balance of the Outer Triangle and remaining within the Inner Triangle to partake in the process of creativity. And now, one final story about activating (or not) the Triangle of Thuse.

Deanna is a college student learning how to write code for websites. Initially she is excited and enthusiastic about the learning process. She does not mind putting in long hours to learn the mumbo jumbo of code, as her brain actively builds a new neural network by firing and wiring countless synapses. Deanna remains calm, optimistic, and takes small steps towards achieving her goal. She faithfully attends class, studies an hour each day, and diligently completes all homework assignments. In the beginning, therefore, Deanna remains focused, able to maintain the balance of her Outer Triangle *and* experience effortless effort inside her Inner Triangle. But then she hits a snag. Suddenly, the seesaw effect between effort and struggle takes over.

"With her Outer Triangle balanced Deanna is able to remain enthusiastic, keeping her Thuse ignited while her process of creativity helps her to more effortlessly problem solve."

Unexpectedly, Deanna is faced with a family emergency and misses a couple of classes. She begins to feel stressed by a potential loss; worry and angst produce chemicals that course through her body. Not only is Deanna in fight, flight, or freeze mode, but her beta brainwaves are on overdrive in a high frequency state. She becomes unable to focus, which causes her to procrastinate. As might be predicted, struggle ensues. Deanna's Outer Triangle is out of balance but in addition, her initial enthusiasm has all but disappeared. Without awareness of the brain's antics, Deanna has unwittingly allowed Dord to cast her passion for learning code out the window. Deanna needs to rebalance her Outer Triangle but she also must rekindle her enthusiasm before being able to move back into the Inner Triangle.

The problem? Deanna has yet to develop a tool kit of techniques to dismantle worry concerning her perceived loss. Also, she is not consciously aware of having shifted from effort to struggle. Having missed so many classes, she feels overwhelmed trying to catch up on assignments. Her predisposition to perfectionism sends her spinning into procrastination. Finally, because her Thuse was not quite rooted in the Inner Triangle, the flame of Deanna's enthusiasm is eventually extinguished.

Increasingly absent from lectures and falling further behind on class assignments, Deanna begins to lose her grasp on the information. She can no longer solve code problems. As a result, Deanna drops the class; her passion for coding will have to wait for another day. Had Deanna previously developed knowledge of, and practice with, the Triangle of Thuse, she might have had different results. How?

Let's rewind Deanna's scenario. In the new version, Deanna understands and practices the concepts of the Triangle of Thuse. She handily develops a tool kit of techniques to help her move through difficult emotions and perceived loss. Deanna's keen awareness of Dord, combined with working hand in hand with Sazy and Rawk, support her through the family crisis. She does not fall for the brain's antics (all those perceptions and beliefs!); instead, she is able to remain in effort rather than being engulfed by struggle. With her Outer Triangle balanced Deanna is able to remain enthusiastic, keeping her Thuse ignited while

"When presented with a coding problem, she can easily enter the Inner Triangle and remain calm, focused, and attentive to her Thuse which she is able to respond to in a matter of seconds."

her process of creativity helps her to more effortlessly problem solve. As a result, Deanna does not drop the college class. In fact, she graduates and finds a job well suited to her interests and skills.

Today Deanna still loves to code and does so successfully, thanks to a strong knowledge base and her continued practice of the Triangle of Thuse. When presented with a coding problem, she can easily enter the Inner Triangle and remain calm, focused, and attentive to her Thuse, which she is able to respond to in a matter of seconds. Moreover, Deanna feels contented by the experience of effortlessness, timelessness, and endless energy as she works on a project. What's left for Deanna?

"The final step would be to operate from the Mind of Thuse."

The final step would be to *operate* from the Mind of Thuse. Deanna could shift from thinking through a problem from within the Inner Triangle into the nonthinking space of the infinite Mind of Thuse. As a result, Deanna would instead effortlessly write code, without thinking, as it poured through her fingertips. Deanna could be coding without a premeditated thought. True, Deanna's facility with coding is based on previously stored memory; however, the difference is that now she would be tapping into the Mind of Thuse that inexplicably helps her write code with flourish and ease. Who knows? Perhaps she'd be the one to write the definitive open source code to solve global warming!

Here's the final word: the Triangle of Thuse helps you develop stillness so that those eureka moments, brilliant insights, and nuggets of wise guidance can be "heard" at any time, in any place—while driving, in the shower, or just walking around the block. Once you start flowing within the Triangle of Thuse, you may want to keep a notebook, sketch pad, or recorder nearby to record ideas. Not only are we able to tap into a source of problem solving and idea flow but also we have the opportunity to transition into the Mind of Thuse.

KNOWING WHAT WE KNOW

We're done. We're out of the rabbit hole. We've burrowed, examined, questioned, and turned theories and philosophies inside out to explore the concept of the multidimensional and powerful Triangle of Thuse. It has been quite a journey. Nevertheless, we have landed. Perhaps even a tad wiser.

"Being in the Mind of Thuse reminds me of the first time I saw a panel of Claude Monet's water lily paintings."

When connected to and working from within the Mind of Thuse, the painter stops thinking about her next paint stroke; the writer stops predetermining his next sentence; the gardener just knows where the next plant should be placed; and … the trekker knows where her foot placement must be, in spite of running down a mountain in the dark. The painter, writer, gardener, and trekker are *thriving*. Having embraced their unique processes of creativity, they are now flourishing when functioning from the Mind of Thuse—that unquantifiable, amorphous space that just knows what it knows without thinking.

Being in the Mind of Thuse reminds me of the first time I saw a panel of Claude Monet's water lily paintings. In that moment, I was simultaneously inspired and awestruck. I will never forget that moment or the painting—so massive, expressive, and out of control. How could a man well into his 80's produce such an explosive, dynamic masterpiece?

In hindsight, based on my own practice of the process of creativity as an artist and writer, I now believe the entire series of water lily paintings emerged from Monet's innate understanding of his own process of creativity. The water lilies are vibrant and teeming with joy. Each paint stroke appears to contain a vibration of enthusiasm—that is, Thuse personified. Further, the paint strokes seem fluid and free from premeditation. In short, Monet appears to be painting from the Mind of Thuse, from the "no-thought" space that vibrates in alignment with all that is.

Yep, I can almost hear your thoughts: "I'm no Monet! He was a masterful genius at his craft." Well, you may or may not be a Monet … and he certainly was a master. And even while you may not produce the work of Monet, you do have the ability to vibrate with enthusiasm and contentment derived from your own inner Thuse. You do have the ability to experience effortlessness, timelessness, and endless energy with not only your endeavors but also your everyday life. You do have the ability to operate from the Mind of Thuse—in which you can have moment-by-moment experiences of trusting the next action without a thought of what that next action might be. Finally, you do have the opportunity to produce your own kind of masterpiece, unique to you and your world.

"You do have the ability to operate from the Mind of Thuse—in which you can have moment-by-moment experiences of trusting the next action without a thought of what that next action might be."

References

Alpha wave. (2008). In *Wikipedia, the free encyclopedia*. Retrieved June 19, 2008, from http://en.wikipedia.org/wiki/Alpha_wave

Aczel, A. D. (2003). *Entanglement*. New York, NY: Penguin Group.

Bekhtereva, N. P. (1988). Dangers and opportunities for change from a physiologist's point of view. In A. Gromyko & H. Hellman (Eds.), *Breakthrough: Emerging new thinking* (pp. 193-198). New York, NY: Walker and Company.

Beta wave. (2008). In *Wikipedia, the free encyclopedia*. Retrieved June 19, 2008, from http://en.wikipedia.org/w/index.php?title=Beta_wave

Bogen, J. (2000). Split-brain basics: Relevance for the concept of one's other mind. *Journal of the American Academy of Psyhoanalysis, 28*(2), 341-369. Retrieved from PEP Archive database. http://search.ebscohost.com.exproxylocal.library.nova.edu/login.aspx?direct=true&db=pph&AN=JAA.028.0341A&site=ehost-live Note: Online article from database.

Bowden, E. M. & Jung-Beeman, M. (2006). Neurocognitive mechanisms of creativity: A toolkit. In Arne Dietrich (Ed.), *Methods, 42*(1), 87-99. Retrieved from http://www.elsevier.com/

Bowers, K.S. (1994). Intuition. In R.J. Sternberg (Ed.), *Encyclopedia of intelligence* (pp. 613-617). New York, NY: Macmillan.

Bowers, K. S., Farvolden, P., & Mermigis, L. (1995). Intuitive antecedents of insight. In S. M. Smith, T. M. Ward, & R. A. Finke (Eds.), *The creative cognition approach* (pp. 27-52). Cambridge, MA: MIT Press.

Boyce, B. (2012, March). Taking measure of the mind. *Shambhala Sun, 20*(4). 42-49 & 81-82.

Browne, M. W. (1997). Signal travels farther and faster than light. *Science News*. Retrieved from: http://www.cebaf.gov/news/internet/1997/spooky.html Jefferson Lab: Newport, VA.

Burnett, F. H. (1911). *The secret garden*. New York, NY: Frederick A. Stokes.

Carter, R. (2009). *The human brain book*. New York, NY: Dorling Kindersley Limited.

Claxton, G., Edwards, L., & Scale-Constantinou, V. (2006). Cultivating creative mentalities: A framework for education. In *Thinking skills and creativity, 1*(1), 57-61. doi: 10.1016/j.tsc.2005.11.001

Conyers, M., & Wilson D. (2010). *BrainSMART: 60 strategies for boosting test scores* (3rd ed.). Orlando, FL: BrainSMART.

Csikszentmihalyi, M. (1990). Flow: The psychology of optimal experience. New York: HarperCollins.

Csikszentmihalyi, M. (1996). *Creativity: Flow and the psychology of discovery and invention.* New York, NY: HarperCollins.

Delta wave. (2008). In *Wikipedia, the free encyclopedia.* Retrieved from http://en.wikipedia.org/wiki/Deltawave

de Salzman, M. (1999). Gurdjieff, G. I. In M. Eliade (Ed.), *The Encyclopedia of Religion.* London: Macmillan Publishing Company. Retrieved from http://www.gurdjieff.org/msalzmann1.htm

Delude, C. M. (2005, October). Brain researchers explain why old habits die hard. *MIT news.* Retrieved from http://web.mit.edu/newsoffice/2005/habit.html

Dietrich, A. (2007). The wavicle of creativity. In Arne Dietrich (Ed.), *Methods, 42*(1-2), 489-490. doi:10.1016/j.ymeth.2007.03.006

Dispenza, J. (2007). *Evolve your brain: The science of changing your mind.* Deerfield Beach, Florida: Health Communications, Inc.

Dobbs, D. (2005, March). Zen gamma. *Scientific American, 16*(1), 9. Retrieved from http://www.scientificamerican.com/article.cfm?id=zen-gamma

Dord. (n.d.). In *The urban dictionary.* Retrieved from http://www.urbandictionary.com/define.php?term=dord

Dorfman, J., Shames, V. A., & Kihlstrom, J.F. (1996). Intuition, incubation, and insight: Implicit cognition in problem solving. In G. Underwood (Ed.), *Implicit cognition.* (pp. 1-23). Oxford: Oxford University Press.

Emoto, M. (2001). *The hidden messages in water.* New York, NY: Atria Books.

Enthusiasm. (n.d.). In *Online Etymology Dictionary.* Retrieved from http://www.etymonline. com/index.php?allowed_in_frame=0&search=enthusiasm&searchmode=none

Fink, A., Benedek, M., Grabner, R. H., Staudt, B., & Neubauer, A.C. (2007). Creativity meets neuroscience: Experimental task for the neuroscientific study of creative thinking. In Arne Dietrich (Ed.), *Methods, 42*(1), 68-76. doi: 10.1016/j.ymeth.2006.12.001

Flett, G. L., & Hewitt, P. L. (2002). Perfectionism and maladjustment: An overview of theoretical, definitional, and treatment issues. In G. L. Flett & P. L. Hewitt (Eds.), *Perfectionism: Theory, research, and treatment* (pp. 5-31). Washington, DC: American Psychological Association.

Geirland, J. (2004). Go with the flow. *Wired Magazine.* Retrieved from http://www.wired.com/wired/archive/4.09/czik_pr.html

Geirland, J. (2006, February). Buddha on the brain: The hot new frontier of neuroscience: Meditation! *Wired Magazine. 14*(2). Retrieved from http://www.wired.com/wired/ar chive/14.02/dalai.html

Goleman, D., Kaufman, P., & Ray, M. (1992). *The creative spirit.* Boston, MA: Dutton Books.

Guna. (2009, April 17). In *Wikipedia, the free encyclopedia.* Retrieved from http://en.wikipedia.org/wiki/Guna

Gura, T. (2008, November). Procrastinating again? How to kick the habit although biology is partly to blame for foot-dragging, anyone can learn to quit. *Scientific American Mind, 19*(6), 26-33. Retrieved from http://www.scientificamerican.com/article. cfm?id=procrastinating-again

Hale-Evans, R. (2006). *Mind performance hacks: Tips & tools for overclocking your brain.* Sebastopol, CA: O'Reilly Media.

Hamachek, D. E. (1978). Psychodynamics of normal and neurotic perfectionism. *Psychology: A Journal of Human Behavior, 15*(1), 27–33.

Hey, T., & Walters, P. (2003). *The New Quantum Universe.* Cambridge, UK: University Press.

Howard, P. J. (2006). *The owner's manual for the brain: Everyday applications from mind-brain research.* (3rd ed.). Austin, TX: Bard Press.

Hudgik, S. (n.d.). *What is Kaizen?* Retrieved from
   http://www.graphicproducts.com/tutorials/kaizen/index.php

James Clerk Maxwell. (2012). In *Encyclopedia Britannica.* Retrieved November 17, 2012 from
   http://www.britannica.com/EBchecked/topic/370621/

Jayaram, V. (n.d.). *Introduction to Hinduism: The triple gunas, sattva, rajas, and tamas.*
   Retrieved from http://www.hinduwebsite.com/gunas.asp

Kihlstrom, J. F., Shames, V. A., & Dorfman, J. (1994). *The relation of implicit memory to
   metacognition.* Paper presented at the meeting of Department of Psychology: Carnegie
   Mellon, 26th Carnegie Symposium on Cognition, Pittsburg, Pennsylvania. Retrieved
   from http://ist-socrates.berkeley.edu/~kihlstrm/Metacognition96.htm

Lauterwasser, A. (2006). *Water sound images: The creative music of the universe.*
   Newmarket, NH: MACROmedia Publishing.

LeDoux, J. (1997, August). *Neal Miller distinguished lecture.* Lecture presented at the meeting of
   the Psychological Association Annual Convention, Chicago, Ill.

Lipton, B. (2008). *The biology of belief.* Carlsbad, CA: Hay House, Inc.

Mavromatis, A. (1987). *Hypnagogia: The unique state of consciousness between wakefulness and
   sleep.* London, UK: Routledge and Kegan Paul.

Missildine, W. H. (1963). *Your inner child of the past.* New York: Simon & Schuster.

Moore, D. W., Bhadelia, R. A., Billings, R. L., Fulwiler, C., Heilman, K. M., Rood, J. &
   Gansler, D. A. (2009). Hemispheric connectivity and the visual-spatial divergent-
   thinking component of creativity. *Brain and Cognition, 70*(3), 267-272.
   doi:10.1016/j.bandc.2009.02.011

Pagels, H. R. (1982). *The cosmic code.* New York, NY: Simon & Schuster.

PBS: NOVA Teachers. (2006). *The science of superstrings.* Retrieved from
   http://www.pbs.org/wgbh/nova/education/activities/3012_elegant_00.html

Pilcher, H. (2004, August). Gene therapy cures monkeys of laziness: Switching off key gene turns
   layabout primates into keen workers. *Nature News.* doi:10.1038/news040809-10

Pychyl, T. A. (2009, September 1). Quirks of the brain: Procrastination's perfect storm. How our brain tricks us into procrastinating. *Psychology Today*. [Web log post]. Retrieved from http://www.psychologytoday.com/blog/dont-delay

Rae-Dupree, J. (2008, May). Can you become a creature of new habits? *The New York Times/ Business*. Retrieved from http://www.nytimes.com/2008/05/04/business/04unbox.html

Rawkin'. (2008). In *The urban dictionary*. Retrieved from http://www.urbandictionary.com/define.php?term=rawk

Raelin, J. A. (2002). I don't have time to think! Versus the art of reflective practice. Reflections. 4(1), 66-79. Retrieved from http://www.ilm.neu.edu/pedagogical/concur rent_reflection/raelin_reflective_practice.pdf

Reiner, P. (2009, November). Meditation on demand. *Scientific American Mind, 20*(6), 65-67. Retrieved from http://lsproxy.austincc.edu/login?url=http://search.ebscohost. com/login.aspx?direct=true&db=pbh&AN=44

Robbins, J. (2008). *A symphony in the brain*. New York, NY: Grove Press.

Ryan, M. J. (2006). *This Year I Will...*. New York, NY: Broadway Books.

Sazy. (2009). In *The urban dictionary*. Retrieved from www.urbandictionay. com/define.php?term=sazy)

Sci. (2012). *Science's top ten eureka moments: Alternating currents*. Retrieved from http://science.discovery.com/brink/top-ten/eureka-moments/eureka-02.html

Seligman, M. E. (2007). *The optimistic child*. New York, NY: Houghton Mifflin Company.

Seng-Ts'an. (n.d.). *Hsin-hsin ming*. Retrieved from http://www.selfdiscoveryportal.com/cmSengTsan.htm

Sousa, D. A. (2006). *How the brain learns* (3rd ed.). Thousand Oaks, CA: Corwin Press.

Stafford, T. & Webb, M., (2005). *Mind hacks: tips & tools for using your brain*. Sebastopol, CA: O'Reilly Media.

Stix, G. (2011, March). The neuroscience of true grit: When tragedy strikes, most of us ultimately rebound surprisingly well. Where does such resilience come from? *Scientific American, 304*(3), 28-33.

Taylor, C., & Laguerre, M. (Producers). (2012). *Joy in the Congo: A musical miracle.* [Television Series]. USA: CBS.

TEDtalksDirector. (2008). *Brian Green: Making sense of string theory.* Retrieved from http://www.youtube.com/watch?v=YtdE662eY_M

Theta wave. (2008). In *Wikipedia, the free encyclopedia.* Retrieved June 19, 2008, from http://en.wikipedia.org/w/index.php?title=Theta_wave

Thompson, E. (2011, June 20). *The narrow, stress-inducing focus of excessive beta brainwaves.* [Web log post]. Retrieved from http://www.iawakeblog.com/2011/06/narrow-stress-inducing-focus-of.html

Wallas, G. (1926). *The art of thought.* Retrieved from http://www.newworldencyclopedia.org/entry/Graham_Wallas

Weber, E. (2007, March 28). *Brain based business. Why perfectionism is bad for the brain.* [Web log post]. Retrieved from http://www.brainbasedbusiness.com/2007/03/why_perfectionism_is_bad_for_t.html

Werbock, J. (2004). Inner octaves and eastern music. *Gurdjieff International Review.* Retrieved from http://www.gurdjieff.org/werbock1.htm

Wilson, D., & Conyers, M. (2010). *Thinking for results: Strategies for increasing student achievement by a much as 30%.* (3rd ed.). Orlando, FL: BrainSMART

Wise, A. (2002). *Awakening the mind: A guide to mastering the power of your brainwaves.* New York, NY: Penguin Group.

LINDA S. SMARZIK

THE STORY BEHIND THE STORY

Photo: Korey Howell

Linda has taught visual design and problem solving with the Visual Communication Department at Austin Community College District for over two decades. During the first decade, questions concerning creativity began to surface as she noticed differences among her students' creative abilities. She began to ask herself: "What process allows some students to access creativity more easily than others?" and "How can individuals more readily tap into the creative process to complete a project or reach a goal?"

In 1999, during a trek in the Nepal Himalayas, long-sought-after answers began to unfold. On the second evening of her journey, she experienced such intense altitude sickness that Linda was told to immediately return down the mountain to the next lodge, two hours away. There was little light left in the evening sky as she and her guide Dawa began running back down the mountain on a crumbling, rocky trail. Earlier in the day Linda had trekked for a full eight hours and, as a result, fatigue had set in. As her footing became uncertain, Linda began to slip and stumble close to the sheer drop-offs. Yet, during that dangerous Himalayan descent, something amazing happened.

Exactly what transpired on that Himalayan mountain range has taken Linda years to sort out. Soon after Linda returned home, she was asked by the local newspaper to write an article about the journey. Although the article went unpublished, the process of writing about the experience got Linda thinking about the connection between her Himalayan experience and the process of creativity.

Linda realized that what had happened during her descent was no different from the experience of a painter effortlessly surrendering to the next paint stroke or a writer letting her fingers fly across a keyboard. Furthermore, she realized this process of creativity or effortlessness does not pertain just to "creative" individuals. Rather, everyone has the ability to tap into their own effortlessness. This realization, this new understanding, now serves as the foundation for Linda's writing, research, and teaching.

Linda's career has taken her in diverse and interesting directions—from Vice President/Creative Director of her own advertising firm to Dean of Computer Studies and Advanced Technology at Austin Community College District. Linda is, in her own words, a "creative geek." Throughout her 30's, she was an artist/painter, participating in a number of juried shows, group shows, and one-woman exhibitions. Then, in her 40's, she began to write about the process of creativity in an effort to convey this concept to her students. Thus, *The Mind of Thuse!!* has emerged.

Visit Linda at www.onebreathvillage.com

CPSIA information can be obtained at www.ICGtesting.com
Printed in the USA
LVOW03s1807140815

450119LV00010B/83/P